THE SACRED AUTUMN

Aging According to Carl Jung

Individuation, Archetypes, Wisdom, Dreams, And Transcendence In Old Age According To Jung

Malcolm J. Austin

Contents

Introduction

At the twilight of life, when shadows grow long and time takes on a new meaning, the human gaze turns inward, seeking in the depths of the psyche the keys to understanding the meaning of existence. On this inner journey, few thinkers have illuminated the mysteries of the aging mind as lucidly as Carl Gustav Jung. His ideas not only revolutionized developmental psychology but also opened new paths for understanding old age as a stage of spiritual transformation, where archetypes and symbols of the collective unconscious manifest with renewed intensity.

This book delves into Jung's vast legacy to explore the sacred dimension of aging. Through its pages, we discover that old age is not merely a biological decline but an alchemical process in which the mature psyche reaches its highest expression. Jungian theories are presented here not as rigid dogmas, but as maps to navigate the uncharted territories of the mind at dusk, inviting deep reflection on the meaning of life in its final stage.

Throughout this journey, we explore key concepts such as individuation, the Wise Old Man archetype, the transcendent function, and the integration of the shadow. We examine how dreams, symbols, and synchronicities take on special meaning in old age, revealing hidden truths of the soul. We also address crucial topics such as loneliness, loss, confrontation with mortality, and the search for transcendence, from a perspective that transcends the individual to encompass the universal.

It is important to note that this book is not intended to be a practical manual or a self-help guide. Instead, it is a deep immersion into the Jungian vision of aging, designed to illuminate the richness and complexity of this vital stage. The text seeks to build a bridge between Jung's ideas and the concrete experiences of those navigating the autumn of life, offering keys to finding meaning and fulfillment in a world marked by constant change.

Beyond the clinical sphere, this book reveals how Jungian wisdom remains relevant in an era that often trivializes or denies the value of old age. His ideas remind us that aging is not merely a medical or social challenge, but a unique opportunity for psychic and spiritual transformation. By understanding old age as a heroic journey toward the wholeness of being, Jung invites us to embrace the fullness of life until its final breath.

In these pages, the reader will find not only a rigorous exposition of Jungian thought but also an invitation to contemplate one's own existence in a new light. As we delve into the mysteries of the aging psyche, we discover that old age is not an end, but a new beginning: the moment when life reveals itself in all its symbolic depth and the human being comes face to face with their highest destiny.

Welcome to this journey into the wisdom of the sacred autumn.

Malcolm J. Austin

Jung and His Later Years

Carl Gustav Jung was born in 1875 in Kesswil, Switzerland, into a family marked by spirituality and scholarship. From an early age, Jung showed a deep fascination with the mysteries of the human mind, immersed in an inner world filled with vivid dreams, visions, and existential reflections. As he grew, this restlessness led him to explore the vast territories of philosophy, religion, and psychology, seeking answers to fundamental questions about the meaning of life and the nature of the soul.

His path led him to the University of Basel, where he delved into the study of medicine and psychiatry. During this period, Jung encountered the revolutionary work of Sigmund Freud, finding in psychoanalysis an initial map to navigate the labyrinths of the unconscious. The relationship between the two thinkers, initially marked by mutual admiration, became a fruitful collaboration that laid the foundation of modern psychology. However, conceptual and personal differences led to an irreparable break, prompting Jung to develop his own vision of the human psyche.

It was in this context that Jung began to forge the central ideas of his thought: the theory of archetypes, the collective unconscious, the process of individuation, and the importance of symbols in psychic life. Through tireless clinical work and deep introspective exploration, Jung discovered that the human mind was not merely a repository of traumas and individual conflicts, but a vast ocean echoing with the voices of history and culture. His travels through Africa, the Americas, and Asia revealed to him the universality of certain symbolic patterns, reinforcing his conviction that a shared dimension of the psyche exists that transcends geographical and temporal boundaries.

But it was in the second half of his life, as he himself entered old age, that Jung began to explore more deeply the mysteries of this crucial stage of existence. Far from viewing aging as mere decline, Jung understood it as a process of psychic transformation, a period in which the mature mind turns inward in search of meaning and transcendence. Through his work with older patients and his own personal experience, Jung discovered that old age is a time of inner harvest, when the fruits of a lifetime of experiences and learning can be integrated into a coherent whole.

In this sense, Jung saw in old age a unique opportunity for individuation—that process of self-realization that leads a human being to become who they truly are. According to his vision, it is at life's twilight that the archetypes of the collective unconscious, such as the Wise Old Man and the Great Mother, emerge most strongly, guiding the individual toward a deeper understanding of themselves and their place in the world. At the same time, Jung emphasized the importance of confronting and integrating the shadow—those dark and rejected aspects of the personality that, if ignored, can become obstacles to psychological growth.

As Jung entered his own golden years, his vision of old age as a journey toward wholeness grew ever more profound and nuanced. In his later writings, he explored themes such as wisdom, spirituality, death, and transcendence, offering a perspective that challenged negative stereotypes about aging. For Jung, old age was not an end but a new beginning—a time when life reveals itself in all its symbolic depth and the human being comes face to face with their highest destiny.

When Carl Gustav Jung passed away in 1961 at the age of 85, he left behind a legacy that has continued to inspire generations of psychologists, thinkers, and spiritual seekers. His ideas about old age as a time of growth and transformation have opened new paths for understanding and fully living this crucial stage of existence. Through his life and work, Jung invites us to embrace the autumn of life with openness, wisdom, and gratitude, recognizing in it a unique opportunity for self-realization and transcendence.

1. The Path to Wisdom

The concept of individuation is defined as the psychological process by which a person attains their fullest sense of self. Rather than being a linear progression, this journey involves a profound transformation, where the conscious and unconscious aspects of the psyche are brought into intentional harmony. Jung describes this path, in "The Relations Between the Ego and the Unconscious" (1928), as a "process of differentiation whose goal is the development of the individual personality." In old age, this process takes on a distinct quality: while the body undergoes inevitable physical changes, the mind is tasked with weaving together life's experiences into a meaningful narrative. The aim is not perfection, but wholeness—to accept what one has been, what one is, and what one may still become, even in the face of life's finitude.

Old age, rather than being defined solely by loss, becomes fertile ground where individuation can flourish with greater authenticity. For Jung, this stage offers a unique opportunity: as external demands—like work and family responsibilities—diminish, an inner space opens up, ideal for facing what he called "the soul's unfinished business." In "Symbols of Transformation" (1912), he observes that vital energy, once directed outward, now turns inward, encouraging a deep dialogue with the unconscious. This introspective movement requires courage: it means facing repressed memories, unfulfilled desires, and disowned aspects of the self. One powerful example is that of a retired businessman who discovered a hidden passion for painting, allowing him to reinterpret his life and legacy and reconnect with his creativity.

Here, it's important to distinguish between chronological aging—marked by physical change—and psychological aging, which involves emotional and spiritual maturity. Jung documented cases of older individuals whose mental vitality defied common stereotypes. One such case involved an 82-year-old woman who found in Stoic philosophy a framework that helped her integrate experiences of loss. Psychological maturity in later life is marked by adaptability, the ability to find meaning in adversity, and openness to new experiences. This kind of maturity isn't tied to age—some young people remain stuck in rigid patterns, while some older individuals continuously reinvent themselves.

Jung's idea of the "second half of life," developed in "The Secret of the Golden Flower" (1929), identifies a turning point around age 40, when the psyche's focus shifts from the external to the internal. While this process begins in midlife, it often reaches its full expression in old age. Jung likens this development to a tree that, after growing upward toward the sky, must now deepen its roots. If the first half of life is spent building an external identity, the second half is about dismantling that identity to reconnect with the Self—the essential core that transcends the ego. Long-term studies, such as Harvard's 80-year longitudinal research, support this idea: people who spent time in introspection and self-exploration in old age reported higher levels of life satisfaction, regardless of physical condition.

Still, the journey is not without obstacles. The fear of death, for example, may appear as anxiety about the void or unresolved matters. Jung suggested confronting this fear through "symbolic amplification," a method of exploring dreams that feature transitional images—like bridges or journeys—to uncover meanings that bring peace. Another common challenge is the loss of social roles. This requires a process of disidentification: letting go of labels like "teacher" or "mother" in order to rediscover a more essential identity. Practices such as meditation, time in nature, or imaginative dialogue with archetypes can support this transition.

In old age, self-knowledge takes on a unique character: it's not about gathering more facts about oneself, but about accepting one's contradictions. Jung recommended keeping a "shadow journal," recording not only achievements but also moments of fear, selfishness, or envy—viewed without judgment. This practice fosters the integration of disowned aspects of the personality. Recent studies from the Berlin Institute of Gerontology show that such practices significantly enhance emotional conflict resolution in later life.

Introspection at this stage is not simply a review of the past, but an attempt to weave a coherent life story. Methods like the "retrospective life line"—which involves identifying key life events, including failures and seemingly minor moments—can reveal patterns and hidden connections. This approach, widely used in gerontological therapy, helps individuals view their lives as integrated wholes.

The distinction between wisdom and knowledge becomes especially relevant here. While knowledge can be accumulated, wisdom emerges from the deep integration of lived experience. Recent neuroscience research shows that older adults often approach ethical dilemmas by activating brain regions involved in holistic thinking, suggesting a more global mode of processing.

The journey toward psychological integration in old age is dynamic and ongoing. It acknowledges the coexistence of light and shadow within each person—and that embracing this duality is essential to achieving wholeness. One case Jung describes is of a monk who, after decades of ascetic life, began dreaming of wild, unrestrained dances. By exploring these dreams, he uncovered a repressed vitality that he was able to integrate into his spiritual practice, achieving a renewed sense of balance.

History, too, offers powerful examples of individuation in old age. Michelangelo, in his seventies, took charge of designing St. Peter's Basilica, imbuing his work with unparalleled spiritual depth. Marie Curie, after the death of her husband, led the Radium Institute with renewed vision. These stories show how old age can be not only a time of facing challenges but of transforming them into tools for inner growth.

The path to psychic integration does not require grand gestures—just the daily courage to explore one's inner world with unflinching honesty. "The afternoon of life should be a celebration of what has been lived, not its denial," Jung wrote, suggesting that death, viewed through this lens, ceases to be a threat and becomes the final transformation of the self—the closing act of individuation on the journey toward wholeness.

2. Demystifying Old Age

A society's view of aging not only shapes expectations for life's later stages but also reveals its underlying fears. In Western culture, the glorification of youth—rooted in 19th-century industrial capitalism—pushed old age to the margins, framing it as a time of decline, unproductiveness, and obsolescence. This perception stands in contrast to anthropological examples from cultures like the Aymara or traditional Japanese communities, where elders are seen as custodians of collective memory and bridges between the human and the transcendent. For Jung, this tension reflects an archetypal conflict: modern societies project their fear of death onto the elderly, yet also view them as bearers of a wisdom they crave but struggle to understand.

These biases have real, measurable consequences. A 2016 Yale University study found that older adults exposed to ageist messaging showed significantly higher risks of cognitive decline—a phenomenon known as "stereotype threat." Internalizing such beliefs creates chronic stress that accelerates biological aging and undermines mental health. Jung referred to this societal constraint as "shrinking the psyche into a limited space," a pattern still evident today in eldercare institutions that limit autonomy and sever individuals from a full sense of identity.

Jung's approach to aging rejects this reductive view, inviting us to see later life as a time of inner harvest. In "On the Psychology of the Unconscious" (1917), he argues that after age 50, vital energy begins to shift away from external ambitions and toward symbolic dimensions of life, unlocking deeper layers of the collective unconscious. This redirection of psychic energy often explains the renewed interest in art, philosophy, or spirituality in later life. One example is a woman who, after years as a nurse, turned to poetry as a way to process repressed experiences—transforming old wounds into creative expression and gaining a deeper understanding of herself.

The difference between the traditional medical model and Jung's psychological perspective is profound. While geriatric medicine tends to focus on managing physical decline—like hearing loss or osteoporosis—Jung believed such limitations could act as gateways to deeper psychological insight. He tells of a man with macular degeneration who, as his vision faded, developed a powerful ability to interpret dreams, relying on intuition and inner perception as his guide to the symbolic world.

The mainstream concept of "successful aging," popular in recent decades, focuses heavily on physical health and independence, while often ignoring deeper dimensions like emotional vulnerability and the integration of the shadow. A recent study in "The Gerontologist" revealed that many older adults labeled as "successful" under these criteria still reported feelings of existential emptiness. Jung's view offers an alternative: embracing loss and limitation as essential parts of emotional and spiritual growth. The goal is not to eliminate dependency but to live with it meaningfully—without losing one's sense of purpose.

The idea that aging equals unproductiveness falls apart when we consider non-economic forms of contribution. In Tzeltal Indigenous communities, elders act as mediators in conflicts and guardians of oral traditions, reinforcing group cohesion. In modern urban contexts, initiatives like "The Legacy Project" at Stanford University demonstrate how intergenerational storytelling can reduce prejudice and strengthen older adults' sense of purpose. Neuroscience confirms that these interactions activate brain areas related to empathy and episodic memory, promoting well-being for all participants.

Wisdom—understood as the deep integration of life experience—finds fertile ground in old age. Brain imaging studies show that older adults tend to use both hemispheres more evenly when facing complex decisions. This ability to hold opposing truths, known in Jungian terms as "coniunctio oppositorum" (the union of opposites), points to the potential for resolving long-standing inner conflicts. For instance, someone who once lived by rigid principles might, in maturity, embrace new values, resulting in a richer, more coherent sense of self.

Emotional resilience in late life does not mean the absence of conflict—it means greater capacity to transform suffering into growth. Research shows that older adults more frequently employ cognitive reappraisal, reframing negative experiences in a constructive light. From a Jungian perspective, "dialogue with the symptom" helps individuals recognize which parts of the shadow are seeking expression through physical or emotional symptoms—thus turning suffering into a path toward self-integration.

To effectively confront ageism, change must occur beyond the personal level. In education, programs like Age-Friendly Universities aim to include older adults in learning environments where their perspectives matter. On a civic scale, projects like Barcelona's age audits assess how urban planning can exclude older populations—then implement inclusive changes. In psychotherapy, narrative reconstruction techniques help people reframe their life stories through archetypal lenses, allowing them to rediscover meaning and redefine identity.

Jung warned that a society that marginalizes its elders loses contact with its own collective unconscious—a reservoir of symbolic and cultural wisdom essential for its evolution. Old age, far from being a terminal state, is a rich and complex phase filled with potential. In "Civilization in Transition" (1957), Jung wrote:

"Only a tree with deep roots can reach great heights. Old age invites us to grow into the depths of the soul, exploring layers that only time can reveal."

This vision not only restores the dignity of later life, but also underscores its vital role as a period of inner transformation—a time when meaning deepens, even as the horizon narrows.

3. The Wise Old Man Archetype

Among the universal patterns that dwell within the collective unconscious, the Wise Old Man emerges as a living bridge between worldly experience and transcendent understanding. This figure, which Carl Jung identified as a "primordial image," represents not merely accumulated knowledge, but the unique convergence of life experience and a deeper, intuitive comprehension that reaches beyond the immediate.

Across mythologies, this archetype appears in diverse yet fundamentally similar forms. In the Nahua worldview, Huehuetéotl, the elderly fire god, symbolizes wisdom that purifies through the cycle of destruction and renewal. In Greek mythology, Proteus—the old man of the sea who holds secret knowledge—embodies adaptability in the face of ever-changing truths, while preserving a core of authenticity. Though rooted in different traditions, these figures share a common thread: the Wise Old Man does not merely transmit information; rather, he transforms consciousness by challenging it to confront essential questions rather than offering fixed answers.

Within analytical psychology, the relationship between this archetype and the Self takes on special significance in old age—a stage in which Jung observed the emergence of what he called the "transcendent function." This often manifests through dreams or meaningful events that prompt the individual to reconcile internal opposites such as reason and intuition, memory and forgetting, tradition and innovation. A compelling clinical example is that of a retired engineer who repeatedly dreamed of an old alchemist mixing substances in a crucible. Inspired by these dreams, he began integrating seemingly unrelated activities—solving differential equations and tending a garden— discovering in both a shared structure of patterns and connections. This case illustrates how the archetype's presence can lead to a synthesis that enriches everyday life.

To consciously embody this archetype requires more than intellectual understanding. Although the Wise Old Man exists as a potential within the collective unconscious, realizing him requires navigating two key dangers: inflation—where one believes themselves to be literally enlightened—and identification, which reduces wisdom to a fixed social role. To avoid these traps, Jung recommended techniques such as active imagination, a method of engaging in an inner dialogue with the Wise Old Man figure. One might, for example, ask him directly: "What aspects of my life am I seeing only superficially rather than deeply?" As described in the "Red Book", this practice allows for meaningful guidance without falling into vanity or rigidity.

The hidden polarity of the archetype—its shadow—also deserves attention. When not integrated consciously, it can manifest in distorted forms such as the Tyrannical Old Man, who uses knowledge to dominate, or the Foolish Old Man, who trivializes wisdom into clichés. A historical expression of this shadow can be seen in aging leaders who, clinging to power, devolve into dictators unable to relinquish control. Jung proposed countering such distortions through a "legacy examination," a reflective exercise that asks whether one's decisions truly benefit the collective—or merely serve the ego.

This archetype also frequently appears in dreams during old age, particularly in times of existential transition. It may take the form of figures offering symbolic objects—a clock without hands, an incomplete map—or ancestors pointing toward alternative paths. A study by the C.G. Jung Institute in Zurich found that 68% of dreams from individuals over 70 included imagery associated with the Wise Old Man, many featuring water elements like wells or underground rivers. These symbols suggest a call to explore the deepest layers of the unconscious in pursuit of integration and renewal.

Integrating the Wise Old Man into daily life requires cultivating what Zen Buddhists call "shoshin", or "beginner's mind." A retired academic, for example, might adopt this attitude by teaching classical texts not as static artifacts, but as living dialogues with the questions of each new generation. This can be supported by practical exercises like the "daily Socratic dialogue," in which one writes down questions that challenge long-held assumptions—for instance: "What beliefs have I maintained out of habit rather than conviction?"

Contemporary expressions of this archetype are found across many domains—not just among famous figures. In Andean communities, the "yatiris", Aymara sages, combine ancient agricultural practices with communal psychological strategies, helping resolve conflict through metaphors drawn from natural cycles. In theoretical physics, Vera Rubin, in her later years, viewed dark matter not as a problem to be solved but as a reminder that the universe favors open questions over definitive answers. These examples show that the Wise Old Man is not a relic of the past but a living presence that continues to find modern expressions.

The central paradox of this archetype is that the more deeply it is embodied, the clearer it becomes that wisdom is not something to possess, but a continuous flow between the personal and the universal. As Jung wrote in "The Archetypes and the Collective Unconscious":

"The old man who believes he has reached the summit discovers only that he is standing on one more step in the infinite stairway of becoming."

4. The Wise Woman Archetype

When a woman crosses the threshold into elderhood, the archetype of the Wise Woman awakens—reconfiguring her relationship with power and wisdom. Far from being a mere extension of earlier roles or a symbol of decline, this figure embodies the alchemy of inner transformation, where the body, now freed from biological cycles, allows the psyche to access deeper dimensions of ancestral knowledge.

The roots of this archetype stretch back to Neolithic societies, where postmenopausal women held key positions in the transmission of both spiritual and practical knowledge. In Çatalhöyük, these women led ceremonies that wove together astronomy and mythology, marking planting cycles with lunar calendars carved into bone. Later, Ireland's "bean feasa"—wise women—were revered as poets, healers, and judges, challenging male monopolies on power. The medieval persecution of witches, which disproportionately targeted women over 50, was not merely religious repression but a systematic attack on a form of female wisdom. Beneath accusations of "flying on broomsticks" lay deep fears of their social mobility and their control over oral contraceptive knowledge passed from woman to woman.

Psychologically, the Wise Woman differs from the wicked witch not in morality, but in the nature of her power. The latter—like Queen Grimhilde in "Snow White"—clings to control through fear, while the Wise Woman acts as a transformative guide. Jungian analyst Clarissa Pinkola Estés recounts the case of a woman who dreamt of an old woman wielding a knife. Through active imagination, she discovered the "weapon" symbolized a scalpel—a call to cut away old beliefs that blocked her creativity. This process reflects the alchemical principle of "putrefactio", in which decay precedes renewal.

In contemporary societies, this archetype continues to evolve. "Maes de santo" in Brazil's favelas blend "Candomblé" practices with community therapy dynamics, addressing the trauma of violence through ritual trance. In science, neurobiologist Marian Diamond, at 72, challenged conventional beliefs about cognitive decline, demonstrating that the brain continues forming new connections through learning. In art, photographers like Francesca Woodman explored older women as symbols of the androgynous, questioning both time and the roles imposed on the female body.

The influence of the Wise Woman is not limited to women. In men's individuation processes, this archetype can soften the rigidity of the "senex"—the aging patriarch—preventing him from becoming authoritarian. Anthropologist Michael Meade documented how Maasai warriors learn to interpret natural signs under the guidance of elder women who blend intuition and tradition in their teaching. In therapy, this archetype is often activated through role-reversal exercises, where men who prioritized logic and career success explore vulnerable aspects of themselves using metaphors of weaving—shifting from building walls to creating nets.

The transformative potential of this archetype is threatened by its shadow: the risk that wisdom decays into bitterness or cynicism. Older women who mock younger generations often carry stories of suppressed talents and unfulfilled aspirations. Another facet of this shadow appears in mothers who control adult children through inherited guilt, perpetuating generational patterns. As mythologist Nor Hall suggests, "unearthing the bones of the Witch"— the remnants of repressed memories—can turn wounds into pedagogical tools for change.

Several practices have been developed to activate this archetype within the psyche. Feminist circles in Latin America use rituals where participants burn lists of internalized duties—such as the need to always be available or to suppress anger—while reciting poetry by writers like Alfonsina Storni. Retrospective menstrual mapping invites postmenopausal women to reflect on their past cycles, not in nostalgia, but to uncover recurring patterns of power. Even in the context of reproductive trauma, such as forced sterilizations, exercises using clay sculptures can reframe the uterus—not as a symbol of loss, but of resilience.

In the political sphere, the Wise Woman is resurging through movements like senior ecofeminism. In the Basque Country, grandmothers block deforestation projects by chanting songs that blend traditional prayers with lessons in biodiversity. In Silicon Valley, retired engineers are hacking algorithms to eliminate gender bias in AI—demonstrating how marginal knowledge can become a form of resistance.

This archetype redefines the very foundations of feminine power, dissolving the false dichotomy between youth and old age. Artist Yayoi Kusama, still obsessively creating her polka-dotted works well into her 90s, embodies this truth: the Wise Woman does not age—she transcends time. Each wrinkle becomes a map of experience that challenges social norms, transforming the end of biological fertility into the beginning of a deeper symbolic creation. As Jung intuited, the feminine—deeply connected to the unconscious—does not rely on

time to renew itself; it draws its strength from
the timeless depths of the soul.

5. Andropause and Menopause

Menopause and andropause transcend biological definitions and unfold as profound processes of transformation in which the body relinquishes its former dominance to symbolism. Jung observed that these transitions, far from being purely physiological, operate as archetypal rites of passage—exchanging literal fertility for a psychic and creative fecundity. In the Dagara communities of Burkina Faso, postmenopausal women are honored as "kpankun"—those who have returned their blood to the earth—becoming mediators between the living and the ancestors. In the Andes, Q'ero men who complete andropause are initiated as "paqos", interpreters of the messages whispered by the "apus"—sacred mountains— through the clouds. These examples affirm that power does not disappear with the loss of fertility or virility; rather, it is redistributed to deeper dimensions.

For both genders, these stages call for a renegotiation of deeply internalized gender archetypes. Analyst Jean Shinoda Bolen describes menopause as the awakening of a latent energy she calls the "postponed Medusa syndrome": the creative force once directed toward biological gestation now channels itself into long-deferred projects. Studies from the Kinsey Institute confirm this creative rebirth, noting that 68% of women between 50 and 65 engage in activities like writing memoirs, starting businesses, or exploring the arts. In men, andropause activates what mythologist Robert Bly called "the king's descent to the underworld": as testosterone wanes, new emotional and spiritual curiosities emerge. In Iceland, older men's circles are reviving plainsong as a practice that weaves together vulnerability and tradition.

The physical symptoms of these processes—hot flashes, night sweats, fatigue—are viewed in analytical psychology as somatic expressions of a psychic birth. Jung described the case of a 49-year-old patient whose hot flashes were accompanied by visions of threads of fire connecting her uterus to the stars. Through active imagination, she uncovered a deep desire to teach astrology, which she went on to do well into old age. For men, what psychiatrist Jed Diamond calls "irritable male syndrome" reflects not just hormonal shifts but a grief for a version of masculinity historically linked to productivity and control. In Māori rituals, this transition is symbolized through carving "tiki"—ancestral figures—with deliberate imperfections, honoring vulnerability as a gateway to wisdom.

During these stages, dreams often reveal alchemical motifs. Women report images of ovens, crucibles, or volcanoes—symbols of inner transformation. For men, dreams of rivers changing course or trees exposing their roots point to a restructuring of identity. One 58-year-old patient dreamed that his prostate expanded into a coral labyrinth. In exploring the image, he realized he needed to abandon his fixation on quick solutions and embrace a more collaborative, organic approach—what he called "coral thinking."

Traditional cultures honor these transitions through rituals that combine release and consecration. Lakota women celebrate the Empty Basket Ceremony: after years of weaving baskets during their fertile years, they burn them upon reaching menopause, along with objects symbolizing outdated roles. In feudal Japan, men entering andropause practiced "nyūdō"—retiring to monasteries to compose "tanka" poetry reflecting on the impermanence of virility. This tradition echoes today in ceramic and watchmaking workshops where older men transform garages into contemplative spaces, shifting from utility to symbolism.

Modern science supports these ancient intuitions. Recent studies show that the postmenopausal brain increases connectivity between hemispheres, enhancing analogical thinking and creativity. In men, andropause activates the anterior insula—a region linked to emotional self-awareness. According to anthropologist Helen Fisher, these neurological changes prepare elders for roles of mentorship, allowing them to integrate experience with innovation in uniquely meaningful ways.

Yet, these processes are not without risks. Jung warned that getting stuck in nostalgia can block the transformative potential of these stages. One patient, determined to maintain a youthful appearance at age 55, repeatedly dreamed of drowning in an icy lake. In analysis, she came to understand that the ice symbolized her resistance to exploring new forms of erotic and emotional expression. As part of her healing, she created a symbolic altar of cold stones, meditating on her more mature desires.

Today, new rites are emerging to support these transitions. In Berlin, women host "Menopause Raves," dancing to techno in dresses stained with henna—ritualizing their inner heat. In Portland, older men engage in "symbolic hunting," using cameras instead of rifles, transforming the instinct to conquer into one of contemplation. These practices do not romanticize aging but embrace its alchemical potential: menopause dismantles the expectation of obligatory motherhood; andropause confronts men with vulnerability—inviting both to forge new myths beyond biological fertility.

These transitions are not mere endings, but deep reconfigurations. Both men and women are called to explore psychic territories that, in Jung's words, expand the boundaries of consciousness and open the door to a form of fertility that transcends traditional notions of time and the body.

6. The Shadow at Life's Sunset

The shadow that accompanies old age is not merely an echo of the past—it is a reflection shaped over time, molded by silences and unclaimed footprints. Jung recognized that, as one nears life's final stage, repressed elements of the unconscious tend to resurface with peculiar intensity. Not as errors, but as missing pieces in a puzzle longing to be completed. Among the Yaghan communities of Tierra del Fuego, this process takes ritual form in the "kina", where elders wear masks made of beech bark representing their deepest shames. During the ceremony, they dance until the group destroys the masks. The act does not aim to banish the shadows, but to honor them as sources of learning and communal cohesion.

Individually, the shadows of old age acquire subtle but powerful hues. A 2021 study from the Oslo Institute of Gerontology found that over 40% of older adults who exhibited conflictive behaviors—stubbornness, hypersensitivity, or social withdrawal—were responding to unresolved emotional wounds. These ranged from family losses to abandoned dreams. One man, enraged by what he saw as "cultural decline," was actually grieving the personal freedom he had sacrificed for family life. A woman who appeared apathetic was masking a long-frustrated spirit of rebellion. In the case of an 80-year-old nun, dreams led her back to forgotten paths: recurring visions of riding wolves inspired her to resume horseback riding, a passion abandoned in youth.

Jung emphasized that reconciliation with the shadow in old age requires a different approach than in youth. While an intellectual lens might suffice at thirty, later life demands a process that reconnects body and mind. Jungian therapist Marion Woodman developed a method called "bone writing", in which elders make wide gestures across paper, allowing the body to express long-silenced memories. In Japan, some care homes practice "dialogue with objects", where elders engage with family relics or photographs, channeling aspects of their shadow into these items. A pocket watch, for instance, might evoke reflections on the fear of time—or of death itself.

Dreams play a central role in this stage as windows into the unconscious. One older man dreamed repeatedly of a black dog devouring his medication. Upon exploring this imagery, he recalled a childhood incident where, under his father's orders, he drowned a puppy. The dream dog symbolized a deep-seated rage toward the medicalization of his current life. In response, he began writing stories about wild animals that healed those who found them—transforming pain into narrative.

The fear of death, Jung said, is the shadow projected forward. Yet not all cultures approach this fear in the same way. Among the Kaluli of Papua New Guinea, elders are trained in dream practices meant to prepare them spiritually for death, invoking images of their ancestors. In more modern settings, initiatives like "death cafés" offer open spaces to speak freely about mortality—transforming taboo into curiosity and shared human connection.

On a societal level, the shadow toward the elderly manifests as ageism. Research from Yale University shows that ageist beliefs are often internalized long before old age arrives, shaping expectations and limiting potential. In the 1970s, the Grey Panthers movement countered these ideas through street theater, where elders reenacted moments of youthful rebellion—reminding the public that the defiant spirit does not fade with age.

To reconcile with the shadow is to transform its energy into creative expression. A moving example comes from Oaxaca, where Mixtec artisans weave with tangled threads they had stored for years—incorporating knots and "mistakes" into unique textile patterns. This principle inspires therapeutic exercises like the "scar collage," where individuals assemble visual pieces combining images of physical and emotional wounds with motifs that highlight their uniqueness.

One striking story involves a former judge who began stealing books at the age of 70. In therapy, he discovered this behavior was a response to a youth constrained by excessive moral rigidity. Over time, he redirected the impulse—donating books to prisons and teaching law to inmates. Similarly, a retired dancer who had lost mobility began choreographing pieces expressed entirely through eyes and hands—communicating with her body in new, profound ways. These stories show how the limitations of age can open unexpected creative doors.

Integrating the shadow does not make elders enlightened beings, nor does it eliminate contradiction. It transforms them into individuals capable of embracing life's paradoxes with embodied wisdom. Like Zen monks who gather dry leaves while laughing at failure, or Sámi grandmothers who turn their mistakes into traditional songs, those who embrace the shadow attain a form of wisdom that needs no display. In the twilight of life, light and darkness merge into a softer glow—a deeper one—that reflects the value of aging with wholeness and awareness.

7. Synchronicity and Aging

Synchronicity, a central concept in Carl Jung's analytical psychology, takes on a unique depth in old age—a stage of life where the rational and the intuitive intertwine in unexpected ways. Jung defined synchronicity as the simultaneous occurrence of events that, while lacking a direct causal connection, hold deep meaning for the person experiencing them. Developed in collaboration with physicist Wolfgang Pauli, the concept stems from the idea that psyche and matter are not separate realms but interconnected expressions of a single reality. In later life, as social identities begin to fade and focus shifts inward, meaningful coincidences emerge as a subtle language revealing hidden links between the personal and the universal.

Contemporary neuroscience offers insight into why such experiences may become more common in later life. Functional MRI studies show that aging brains tend to activate more integrated neural networks—especially in areas like the medial prefrontal cortex and anterior insula—regions associated with synthesizing experience and intuitive insight. This heightened connectivity allows older adults to perceive patterns that may go unnoticed earlier in life. One telling case involves a 72-year-old woman who, while contemplating a move to a retirement home, began repeatedly noticing the number 23—the age at which her son had passed away. These seemingly random encounters led her to channel her grief into creating a storytelling workshop for seniors, linking her personal loss with collective memory.

In old age, the collective unconscious and its symbols often find powerful expression through dreams and meaningful events. Jung observed that, during existential transitions, older individuals frequently report dreams featuring universal symbols like bridges, rivers, or keys—motifs found in myths and cultural stories across time. One man, at 68, dreamed of a ferryman offering to help him cross a stormy lake. This dream catalyzed a reconciliation with his estranged brother after decades of silence. The image of the ferryman—present in myths from Charon in ancient Greece to Hraf-haf in

Egypt—acted as a symbolic bridge between his family conflict and an archetypal wisdom about life's closing chapters.

Cultivating the ability to perceive synchronicities involves practices that blend careful observation with active symbolic reflection. A valuable technique is the use of a "psychic echo journal", in which coincidental events are recorded alongside the emotions and associations they evoke. For instance, if someone, while thinking about a lost friend, hears a song they used to share and later receives a surprise call from that friend, reflecting on the sequence can reveal a deeper narrative. This method, used in gerontological therapy, supports what Jung called the "transcendent function"—the ability to integrate the unexpected into a coherent life story.

In old age, intuition sharpens as a synthesizing tool enriched by decades of experience. Unlike the more reactive intuition of youth—focused on avoiding immediate risks—mature intuition becomes reflective and strategic. Studies from the Max Planck Institute have shown that older adults resolve ethical dilemmas by activating brain regions linked to both episodic memory and future planning, allowing them to detect deeper patterns in seemingly random events. One example involves a retired teacher who, while reflecting on her life's purpose, received multiple messages from former students in the same week, thanking her for her impact. These encounters inspired her to create an intergenerational mentoring group, reimagining her role beyond the classroom.

Synchronicities can also play a key role in decision-making, helping to counteract the tendency to overanalyze. A Harvard study found that older adults who incorporated meaningful coincidences into their decision-making process reported greater satisfaction, as they combined rational, emotional, and intuitive inputs. One widower, unsure whether to sell or stay in his home, stumbled upon a vase identical to one his late wife collected. The discovery led him to transform the house into a ceramics studio in her honor, turning memory into creative purpose.

To make use of such experiences, tools are needed that translate symbolic insights into tangible action. One such tool is "amplified active imagination", which encourages engaging with symbolic content from meaningful events through creative expression—like drawing or writing. For example, an elderly man who repeatedly dreams of migratory birds may paint them in watercolor as a way of exploring what areas of his life call for change or renewal. Another method, "synchronicity mapping", draws timelines connecting key life events to their associated coincidences, helping to reveal meaningful patterns that support a coherent life narrative.

However, there's a risk in attributing deep meaning to mere chance, mistaking emotional projections for true synchronicity. To guard against this, Jung proposed the "principle of affective resonance", which holds that genuine synchronicity always provokes an emotional jolt and shifts one's perception of reality. For instance, a woman who sees butterflies frequently during chemotherapy and interprets them as symbols of hope might explore whether butterflies have surfaced during other pivotal moments in her life. This approach helps distinguish between the anecdotal and the truly meaningful.

Synchronicity in aging is not merely a mystical comfort—it's an invitation to inhabit a deeply interconnected universe, where even the smallest details can reveal a greater meaning. More than just an aesthetic or spiritual curiosity, it is a way of participating consciously in the symbolic fabric of existence—illuminating the path toward a deeper understanding of life.

8. The Hero's Journey in Old Age

The archetypal structure of the "monomyth", described by Joseph Campbell as a narrative pattern that spans cultures and time periods, finds its most profound expression in old age. At this stage, the hero no longer slays dragons or conquers distant lands. Instead, the battle turns inward—toward the shadows that surface in the twilight of life. Carl Jung, in his exploration of universal archetypes, observed that the process of individuation in later adulthood mirrors the stages of the hero's journey. However, he introduced a crucial shift: the conflict no longer lies in the external world but in the intimate landscape of memory, acceptance, and ego transcendence.

In this phase, the "call to adventure" doesn't arrive dramatically. It comes quietly, through retirement, the death of loved ones, or physical decline. These experiences compel the shedding of an identity forged over decades. A 70-year-old businessman, upon being diagnosed with Parkinson's, faced more than a disease—he faced the collapse of his self-image as a figure of control and action. This crisis—akin to the hero's refusal of the call—led him into what Jung called the descent into the cave of the unconscious. In that dark space, he discovered that his real strength was not in asserting control, but in learning to adapt to uncertainty.

The trials of the elder hero don't require extraordinary physical feats. The true challenge is to reshape the meaning of life. It means accepting help without shame, making peace with the past, and finding beauty in vulnerability. A long-term study from Stanford University showed that older adults who reinterpreted their limitations as opportunities for personal growth demonstrated greater emotional resilience. One woman in a wheelchair transformed her perceived restriction into a symbol of dignity by hosting literary gatherings in her home—proving that physical limitations can coexist with a boundless spirit.

On this journey, the mentor is often no longer an external figure. More commonly, it appears as a voice from the unconscious—a projection of the Self archetype emerging in dreams or synchronicities. A 78-year-old widow, after years of isolation, began dreaming of her grandmother, a healer from her childhood, who taught her how to use medicinal herbs. Upon researching, she discovered those very plants growing in her garden. This dream encounter inspired her to start a therapeutic herb garden, rekindling her sense of purpose and improving her emotional well-being. Neuroscientific research confirmed that working with soil lowered her amygdala activity—linked to fear—and strengthened connections between the hippocampus and prefrontal cortex, areas associated with memory and meaning.

The most critical stage of the elder's journey is the confrontation with mortality—what Jung called the "dark night of the soul." Many older adults describe symbolic encounters with a younger version of themselves—a "double" who questions the paths not taken. A retired architect, hospitalized with pneumonia, described vivid dialogues with his 25-year-old self, who confronted him about abandoning his artistic aspirations for a more secure career. This inner reckoning led him to fund scholarships for young artists, transforming remorse into a meaningful legacy.

The return of the elder hero doesn't bring back a magical object, but a new understanding of time. Cultural gerontologists have observed that older people who frame their lives as epic narratives—with conflicts, villains, and redemption—develop a temporal perspective that unites past, present, and future. A historian who had lost his short-term memory began writing poems that wove together childhood memories from the postwar era with present moments. These poems, later adapted into plays by his grandchildren, showed how a life told with meaning can resonate across generations.

Modern myths continue to mirror this phase of the journey. In "The Iron Lady", Margaret Thatcher, in old age, converses with the ghost of her husband—undertaking an underworld journey that softens her pride. Similarly, a 90-year-old retired union leader, after reconciling with former political adversaries, embodied the hero archetype by transforming past rivalries into bridges of cooperation.

As a therapeutic tool, the heroic model can help older adults reframe their life stories. In reminiscence workshops, participants are invited to identify personal symbols—stolen treasures, talismans of strength, or dragons defeated. One Holocaust survivor illustrated his story by drawing a handkerchief that had protected him like a shield and described his scars as emblems of an epic battle. This exercise not only helped him reconstruct his narrative but also activated brain regions associated with reward processing and emotional resilience.

The elder hero's journey doesn't end with death but with the transmission of their personal myth to the collective. Like the imperfect circles painted by Zen masters, each life becomes an open story—unfinished yet deeply inspiring to those who follow. In this way, aging transcends decline; it becomes a transformation that immortalizes lived experience in a legacy that continues to echo through others.

9. Emerging Archetypes in Old Age

In today's world, old age transcends traditional archetypes like the Wise Elder or the Crone, reshaping itself within a landscape where longevity intersects with global crises and profound social change. These new archetypal patterns emerge as collective responses to unprecedented challenges—technological alienation, environmental urgency, and the redefinition of legacy in an era driven by speed. Carl Jung foresaw that the collective unconscious evolves with each era, and in this age of extended lifespans, the archetypes of old age serve as symbolic tools for navigating existential terrain that remains largely unmapped.

"The Fractal Elder" represents the ability to perceive universal patterns within personal experience. Unlike the classical Sage who preserves immutable truths, this archetype reveals how individual life stories resonate with broader social dynamics. A former banker, reflecting on his workaholism, created a workshop linking economic cycles to Greek myths of greed and moderation. Recent neuroimaging studies show that such practices activate the temporoparietal junction—an area of the brain that integrates diverse perspectives. The aging brain, in this sense, demonstrates a unique capacity to reconcile the individual with the collective, the specific with the universal.

"The Weaver of Time" emerges in women whose lives were fragmented by multiple roles and who, in later life, discover ways to weave those timelines into richer, more layered narratives. A retired engineer created tapestries using computer cables intertwined with yarn dyed by her grandchildren—materializing the convergence of her technological career and emotional heritage. This archetype reflects the sustained synaptic plasticity found in older adults, especially in brain networks responsible for autobiographical integration. Activities like weaving, which merge procedural memory and conceptual thinking, strengthen these neural pathways and help connect the many layers of lived experience.

"The Digital Nomad" illustrates how technology can redefine physical decline as symbolic exploration. In Japan, a group of octogenarians uses virtual reality to revisit places from their youth, sharing their stories through intergenerational broadcasts. This practice activates the Gratton circuit, a neural network that connects spatial memory with imaginative projection—allowing tangible losses to transform into restorative emotional landscapes. Far from being a mere distraction, virtual exploration opens new doors to symbolic healing and intergenerational connection.

"The Alchemist of Chaos" stands as a transformer of both material and emotional remnants from the past. A former oil executive in Norway led a project to convert decommissioned offshore platforms into artificial reefs. Inspired by the alchemical process of dissolving the old to crystallize the new, this initiative activates the lateral habenula, a brain region linked to learning from failure. This archetype embodies the capacity to transmute obsolete identities into meaningful contributions, merging historical experience with contemporary demands.

"The Quantum Bridge" symbolizes the union of seemingly irreconcilable worlds. In India, a retired physicist teaches advanced string theory through tribal dance, connecting science and spirituality through the shared language of vibration. This archetype aligns with neural superfluidity—a phenomenon in which the aging brain forms novel connections between disparate concepts. It reveals how traditional opposites, like reason and intuition, can be understood as complementary poles on the same spectrum.

"The Cartographer of Collective Shadows" transforms generational trauma into maps for social healing. In Latin America, women who survived dictatorships have created interactive installations where everyday objects—stopped clocks, censored letters— become symbols that educate younger generations about historical memory. This approach stimulates what neuroscientists call "epigenetic empathy", a phenomenon where emotional resonance transcends direct experience, enabling deeper intergenerational understanding.

"The Existential Hacker" challenges conventional narratives of aging through acts of creative subversion. In Berlin, a collective of elderly people with Parkinson's developed a gestural language based on their tremors, turning what is typically seen as a deficit into a form of artistic expression. This approach—blending vulnerability and aesthetics—has been shown to reduce physiological stress while strengthening emotional and social resilience.

These archetypes are not fixed categories but reflections of the fluidity of human experience and the transformative potential of aging. Tools like "transgenerational archetypal mapping" help uncover recurring patterns in family histories, showing how archetypes evolve over time. At the same time, "psychic update rituals", such as the use of augmented reality, allow elders to interact with these emerging figures in symbolic spaces—exploring new ways to reinterpret their legacy.

In a time of existential disorientation, these archetypes serve as provisional guideposts. Their value lies in offering elders not just a mirror of their experience, but a canvas on which to redraw it—affirming old age as a creative and meaningful phase of life. In their hands, the chaos and uncertainty of the present become raw material for the myths that will guide future generations.

10. The Alchemy of Aging

Aging, understood through the lens of alchemical metaphor, proposes a transformation of the ordinary into the transcendent—a process Carl Jung reinterpreted from medieval hermetic texts. In this framework, the three fundamental stages of the alchemical work—"nigredo", "albedo", and "rubedo"—transcend their chemical origins to become symbolic maps of psychological change. Associated with the colors black, white, and red, these stages do not merely describe material phenomena but represent the spiritual evolution that defines mature life. Each phase reflects an internal process of dissolution, purification, and synthesis that reveals the essence of a fully lived life.

"Nigredo", or blackening, marks the beginning of this transformation. It corresponds to the collapse of the structures that once defined identity. This disintegration is not limited to physical decline or the abandonment of social roles—it also involves the unraveling of what Jung called "the persona," the mask that mediates our relationship with the external world. A 2023 study from Leiden University, involving 1,200 older adults, found that over 70% of people aged 65 to 75 experienced a period of existential disorientation—a deep questioning of the elements that once defined them: profession, material success, family roles. This collapse, known in alchemical texts as "putrefactio", does not aim to destroy but to expose what is essential. Jung illustrated this through the case of a retired diplomat who, after experiencing panic attacks, had visions of an eagle plucking out its own feathers. Symbolically, the bird represented her professional identity, and its self-stripping reflected the necessary "nigredo" that opened the path to a more authentic self.

As loss is assimilated and resistance to change begins to soften, one enters the stage of "albedo", or whitening. This phase involves a re-signification of personal narrative, where memories are no longer fixed points but malleable material. A study by King's College London found that during this stage, there's increased activation of the inferior frontal gyrus—a brain region linked to reappraising experiences. A striking example comes from a retired nurse who, while sorting through old family photos, confronted long-avoided memories. Instead of viewing them as irreparable failures, she reframed them as chapters of strength, seeing herself not as a victim of circumstances but as the author of a complex, resilient life. "Albedo" becomes a space for self-forgiveness—a reconciliation with past versions of oneself that made choices from fear or ignorance.

The process culminates in "rubedo", or reddening—the stage of integration. It represents the union of psychic opposites—reason and intuition, strength and vulnerability, memory and forgetting—into a transformative synthesis. Just as alchemists believed that combining fire and water could produce the philosopher's gold, this phase unites once-conflicting elements into coherence. A project at the MIT Media Lab explored this through "alchemical biomimicry," where older adults mimicked natural processes like crystallization or decomposition through creative exercises.

The result was a marked increase in neural connectivity, suggesting that embodying nature's transformative patterns can foster greater internal harmony. One notable case involved a former factory worker who, inspired by the fractures in melting ice, began writing haikus that turned past regrets into poetic art—transforming emotional scars into creative insight.

At the heart of this entire journey lies the "prima materia", the raw emotional material accumulated throughout life. Jung recounted the story of a widowed farmer who transformed his grief into a creative ritual, expressing his pain through metaphor and rediscovering his sense of existence. This embodies the core alchemical principle of "solve et coagula"—to dissolve rigid interpretations and reorganize them into narratives that nourish well-being. The perspective that comes with age allows this psychic distillation, helping the past be seen not as a series of irredeemable mistakes, but as fuel for growth.

Yet the path to integration is not without its challenges. One of them is "enantiodromia", a Jungian concept describing how extremes eventually give rise to their opposite. This principle appeared in the case of a feminist academic who, after decades fighting gender stereotypes, began dreaming of herself sewing Victorian dresses. Upon exploration, she realized her youthful rejection of tradition had hidden a deep fascination with textile history. The insight led her to create artistic installations combining antique corsets with quotes from Simone de Beauvoir—reconciling past and present, activism and tradition. This resolution illustrates the law of the "unus mundus": the creative integration of seemingly opposed elements into a unified whole.

Alchemical symbols find tangible application in contemporary practices. The "ouroboros", the serpent that devours itself, is reimagined in therapies where elders write letters to their younger selves and burn them in symbolic closure—using the ashes to fertilize community gardens. Similarly, the "athanor", the alchemical oven, is translated into movement-based art where physical pain becomes expressive dance. One group of people with arthritis developed choreographies inspired by their bodily limitations, transforming discomfort into beauty.

The true "philosopher's stone" of aging is not a physical object but the capacity to reinterpret life as a continuous experiment. A recent study in "The Journal of Aging Studies" found that older adults who describe their lives in terms of hypotheses, lessons, and discoveries experience greater resilience in the face of physical decline. Their stone lies not in achieving perfection but in accepting life as a laboratory of meaning, where mistakes and triumphs are woven into one continuous tapestry. Like the mercurial waters of alchemical lore, the wise elder learns to inhabit contradictions—celebrating what's been achieved while honoring what's been lost, caring for the body without fearing its end, and sharing knowledge without imposing it. Their true work is the art of holding paradoxes until they reveal their hidden unity—like a seed that

must first dissolve in darkness before it can
bloom.

11. Dreams and Aging

In the final stage of life, dreams become a coded language of the unconscious—a space where the personal and the universal intertwine with striking intensity. Carl Jung believed that while the body deteriorates, the psyche finds in dreams a channel to express its vitality, transcending physical limitations. The neurophysiological changes of aging—such as reduced deep sleep (NREM) and fragmented REM—do not diminish the symbolic power of dream imagery. On the contrary, they alter how dreams are perceived and recalled. More frequent micro-awakenings create easier access to these visions, making old age a fertile time for deep dialogue with the unconscious. In this space, dreams are not merely reflections of accumulated memory, but bridges to the existential questions that define the present.

Recurring themes in the dreams of older adults often center around universal symbols: journeys, ancestral figures, or thresholds like doors and train stations. A longitudinal study conducted by the Zurich Institute of Depth

Psychology, based on 2,300 dreams from individuals aged 65 to 90, identified patterns reflecting the psychic work of integrating a complete life. Nearly half of the dreams involved activities such as sorting objects or packing bags—images symbolizing the effort to reorganize experience. A significant portion also featured conversations with younger versions of the dreamer, which Jung interpreted as the psyche's attempt to reconcile fragmented identities across time. These nocturnal narratives express a yearning to unify past and present into a coherent whole.

The technique of "symbolic amplification", which aims to expand the meaning of dream imagery, takes on special resonance in later life. One example comes from a 78-year-old man who repeatedly dreamed of an hourglass whose neck was too narrow to let sand pass. Beyond the obvious association with time, the image reflected his sense of unprocessed experiences blocking acceptance. In therapy, he was guided to sketch variations of the hourglass while recounting moments in which he felt trapped. The exercise activated brain regions linked to autobiographical memory and cognitive flexibility, illustrating how conscious engagement with symbolic images can rewire deeply ingrained patterns.

Recurrent dreams in old age often point to unresolved conflicts that gain urgency in the face of mortality. An 82-year-old woman dreamed of a ship leaving without her from a childhood dock. Upon analysis, the ship symbolized postponed opportunities—like emigrating or pursuing art. Through "dream updating", she reimagined the dream while awake and saw herself boarding the ship, finding blank canvases on deck that inspired her to begin painting. In this way, she transformed persistent anxiety into a creative project, showing how dreams can catalyze symbolic closure and newfound purpose.

The "compensatory function" of dreams becomes more pronounced when the conscious identity grows rigid. A retired judge, obsessed with control, repeatedly dreamed of being a dervish, spinning until he dissolved into air. This was not escapism, but a needed counterbalance to his hyper-rational mindset—an invitation to emotional fluidity. Working with the dream activated brain regions associated with body awareness and empathy, allowing for a novel integration of physical and emotional experience.

Even in cases of cognitive decline, dreams can play a significant therapeutic role. In individuals with early-stage dementia, where episodic memory begins to fade, dreams often retrieve emotional memories from childhood. In elder care centers, programs based on this principle use sensory elements linked to dream content to anchor autobiographical fragments in the present. If a resident dreams of orchards or rural landscapes, those settings are recreated using tactile and olfactory stimuli, helping to slow disconnection from the self. Research from the University of Heidelberg supports the idea that dreams can serve as portals to a sense of personal continuity.

Technology is also beginning to support dream work in old age. Apps like "Oneironaut" allow users to record dreams upon waking, analyzing recurring patterns and key symbols. For users with tremors, interfaces translate their movements into digital strokes, turning dreams into abstract visual art. These tools not only preserve dream content, but also offer tangible ways to explore and reinterpret the inner world.

Jung cautioned against taking dreams too literally—especially in old age. A dream of falling might seem to reflect fear of death, but could equally express a longing to let go of social roles. The dreamer's life context is key to understanding its meaning. One retired businessman, haunted by dreams of falling with broken parachutes, discovered the frayed cords symbolized his attachment to outdated professional identities. By freeing the image of its symbolic burden, he redefined his sense of purpose beyond material success.

In life's final moments, dreams often merge the personal with the transpersonal. Accounts from hospice patients describe eternal gardens or choirs of unfamiliar voices—images that, according to analytical psychology, signal psychic preparation for death. EEG studies have recorded persistent theta activity during REM sleep in these stages, suggesting the brain may explore states of consciousness beyond conventional dualities, helping ease the transition into the unknown.

Dream work in old age does not seek definitive answers, but fosters a spirit of openness toward the mysteries of the psyche. Each dream image, however fleeting, contributes to the process of individuation—reminding us that even in the twilight of life, the symbolic richness of the unconscious continues to unfold in unexpected ways.

12. The Body as the Temple of the Aging Soul

In old age, the body reveals itself as a map—etched with the topography of decades lived. Every fold, scar, and stiffness is a visible trace of the existential journey, a palimpsest where the meeting of psyche and flesh is written. Carl Jung saw these marks as expressions of individuation, where the body mirrors the ongoing dialogue between the unconscious and consciousness. Unlike in youth—when the body is often used as a tool to influence the outer world—aging invites a more contemplative relationship with one's physical being. Recent studies in neurophenomenology show that this stage of life brings heightened interoceptive awareness, a clearer perception of the heartbeat, breath, and circulation. This isn't hypochondria—it's an unexpected access point to deeper layers of the unconscious, linking the emotional and the physical in powerful ways.

Jung's concept of "corpus animatum" highlights how archetypes manifest in the physiology of the body. A study from the

Institute of Medical Psychology in Heidelberg revealed that patients with rheumatoid arthritis activate specific regions of the insular cortex when viewing images of their inflamed joints—suggesting that these brain areas process not only physical pain but repressed emotions. Jung associated such conditions with the "Senex archetype"—a rigid psyche manifesting as joint stiffness. Therapies incorporating active imagination, where patients personify their joints as mythological figures, have been shown to reduce inflammation and markers like C-reactive protein, according to studies in "Psychosomatic Medicine". This approach not only alleviates pain but restores a sense of psychological fluidity.

The "skin", as the boundary between inner and outer worlds, takes on symbolic prominence in aging. It becomes a canvas that holds stories of rejected or longed-for contact. Research in psychosomatic dermatology has found that eczema tends to worsen during emotional conflict, and that age spots often appear in areas tied to specific sensory memories. In Switzerland, "dermographic mapping" programs invite patients to draw on their skin the life events associated with each mark. One man, for example, reinterpreted an abdominal surgery scar as a symbol of emotional rebirth after the loss of his son—and experienced a significant reduction in chronic pain. Functional MRI images confirmed increased activity in emotional processing areas of the brain after this symbolic reframing.

"The voice", often overlooked as a transformative medium, changes in old age in ways that go beyond acoustics. While higher tones may fade, lower frequencies activate brain regions tied to emotional memory and introspection. Techniques like "formant singing", where elders sustain tones that resonate in specific bone cavities, stimulate neurogenesis in the hippocampus and enhance connectivity between the cerebellum and amygdala. Documented in the "Journal of Voice", these methods have shown promise in Parkinson's patients—restoring not just brain function but a sense of dignity and self-expression.

The "digestive system", which Jung referred to as the "enteric brain," reflects unprocessed psychic conflict. Recent research links disruptions in gut microbiota with depressive states in elders, suggesting that certain microbes may correspond to the integration—or repression—of aspects of the self. "Psychobiotic diets", tailored through dream analysis, have been shown to ease chronic intestinal syndromes, revealing the tangible impact of body–mind reconciliation.

"Bones and joints" embody the tension between structure and flexibility, between holding on and letting go. Viewed symbolically, osteoporosis may reflect a resistance to releasing outdated psychological constructs. In "osteodrama workshops", participants act out their bone cells as forces in dialogue—experiencing not just improved bone density, but also softer, more fluid family dynamics. Brain scans have shown that these practices activate regions involved in processing body metaphors, highlighting the connection between symbolic change and physical regeneration.

The "aging heart", with its arrhythmias and pauses, beats in time with emotions accumulated over decades. "Cardiac biofeedback" techniques combined with active visualization—such as imagining mandalas or archetypal symbols—have been shown to improve heart function and guide individuals toward a deeper integration of life experience.

"Breathing", the bridge between the voluntary and the automatic, acquires profound symbolism in old age. Practices like "fractal exhalation", inspired by the patterns of aging tree branches, teach elders to accept the gradual decline of lung capacity as a form of wisdom in sufficiency. Neuromonitoring shows these practices stimulate brain areas linked to emotional acceptance and inner balance.

"Chronic pain", common in later life, often prompts profound questions about the mind–body relationship. The theory of "psychic neuromas" suggests that certain persistent pains encapsulate unprocessed trauma. "Somatic rewriting therapies", which combine symbolic storytelling with brain stimulation, are helping reduce reliance on painkillers in elder care. One woman with diabetic neuropathy reimagined her foot pain as "roots searching for fertile soil"—a metaphor that reduced her discomfort and activated neural networks related to self-image.

Even the "aging brain" retains remarkable plasticity and potential for reinvention. Practices like "oneiric tai chi", in which movements are based on dream sequences, have been shown to regenerate neural connections in people over 75. In this way, each gesture or stiffness becomes a unique expression of a life deeply and authentically lived.

The aging body is not a burden—it is the most faithful reflection of a soul still learning. In its fragility lies the strength of a life that has shed the superficial to embrace the essential. Every mark, every limitation, sings a hymn of acceptance and reveals, in its vulnerability, the beauty of a human being who has learned to fully inhabit their mortal temple.

13. Modern Rituals for Honoring Aging

In post-industrial societies, the invisibility often surrounding aging is increasingly counterbalanced by the invention of contemporary rituals that restore meaning to this vital stage of life. These acts do not aim to replicate ancient traditions, but instead craft new symbolic languages that engage with today's technological, ecological, and communal landscapes.

In Japan, gerontological clinics have developed the "shukou", a ceremony in which elders share their memories, which are then transferred to artificial intelligence systems— creating digital avatars that preserve and continue their personal narratives. Rather than resisting mortality, this process addresses personal legacy, allowing conscious editing of the past to reshape its significance.

In urban environments, artistic initiatives like "generational mapping" have emerged as creative responses to intergenerational disconnection. In Berlin, elders project their life stories onto building façades using laser technology, transforming postwar memories into luminous patterns that respond to weather conditions. These experiences not only reconcile personal and collective memory, but also stimulate brain regions associated with memory and future planning—strengthening historical belonging and temporal continuity.

The hyperconnectivity of the digital age has also inspired "rituals of technological disconnection", such as secular monasteries in Portugal that offer "archetypal detox ceremonies". Over the course of several weeks, participants repurpose their digital devices as altars, using them to explore personal archetypes via augmented reality. Tools developed at institutions like MIT overlay mythological avatars onto selfies, helping individuals identify and transform outdated behavioral patterns.

In rural settings, rituals like "kompostage de soi" integrate human aging with the cycles of planetary regeneration. At communal farms in France, participants bury personal objects alongside organic waste, observing how decomposition nourishes new crops. This symbolic act reinforces a connection to natural rhythms—and interestingly, also correlates with physiological change: greater diversity in gut microbiota, which is linked to better acceptance of mortality.

Elsewhere, the "reinvention of time as sacred experience" finds expression in circles of "applied chronomagic". In California, groups use algorithms and portable sundials to visualize their remaining lifespan as interactive chromatic landscapes. These practices integrate achievements and regrets into symbolic tapestries, reducing existential anxiety by activating brain areas linked to positive anticipation.

Even within medical contexts, routine procedures are beginning to incorporate ritualistic elements. In Swedish hospitals, insulin injections are preceded by "micro-ceremonies", in which patients draw alchemical symbols on their skin—transforming clinical acts into empowering moments of self-care.

Recent studies suggest these practices reduce treatment resistance and help shift the narrative from deterioration to transformation.

"Living legacy rituals" have gained traction through technologies like blockchain. These platforms enable the bequeathing of not only material assets, but also gestures, recipes, or breathing patterns, encoded as interactive digital assets. A notable case in Seoul involved the creation of an NFT documenting an elder's tea-making ritual, preserving his motions and traditions in a format accessible to future generations.

Urban loneliness has also prompted innovative approaches such as "portable temples of experience". Equipped with sensors and projectors, these mobile sanctuaries transform ordinary spaces into temporary shrines—where light patterns triggered by the user's heartbeat foster an immediate sense of emotional connection. Studies in New York elder care facilities show these interventions boost oxytocin levels, deepening emotional bonds with one's environment.

Challenging linear narratives of time, "quantum biography workshops" invite participants to reconstruct their life stories in non-linear formats—linking past and future events into simultaneous constellations. Research from the University of Buenos Aires shows that this approach enhances autobiographical integration by activating brain regions essential for time perception.

In ecological contexts, initiatives like "Future Roots" in Canada interweave human experience with the life of trees. Here, elders plant and tend forests whose growth they observe through virtual reality, becoming symbolic bridges between their legacy and the generations to come. This act reframes fear of death into a nourishing connection with life's greater cycles.

In their diversity and depth, these rituals transform the challenges of aging into opportunities for genuine meaning. By re-enchanting the everyday through purposeful practices, they offer individuals concrete tools to contemplate the fullness of their legacy and the creative potential still within them. In this light, aging ceases to be a time of loss and becomes a space for continuous creation.

14. Solitude as a Path

Old age offers a peculiar kind of space—an inner retreat that should not be mistaken for emptiness, but rather understood as fertile ground where the soul, in the Jungian sense, is reshaped. For Carl Gustav Jung, it was crucial to distinguish between involuntary isolation, which plunges the individual into despair, and conscious solitude, chosen as a vehicle for transformation. The latter unfolds as a deep space for introspection, free from the roles and commitments that once shaped daily life.

Recent studies from the C.G. Jung Institute in Zurich have shown that older adults who engage in these periods of active solitude display greater activity in the medial prefrontal cortex, the area of the brain associated with autobiographical integration. This confirms Jung's insight: in reflective silence, scattered experiences reorganize into narratives that bring coherence and meaning to one's identity.

The archetype of the Hermit, a recurring figure in mythology and spiritual traditions, aligns with this perspective. Rather than renouncing the world, the Hermit symbolizes a strategic withdrawal for clarity and understanding. In Greek mythology, the figure of Geras—the old man who lit the days with his lamp—illustrates the ability to find light in solitude's seeming darkness. This idea transcends cultures. For example, Zen Sōtō monks alternate solitary meditation with brief communal gatherings during their "sesshin", reflecting a balance between introspection and connection.

Jung documented a compelling case: a woman who, after years of paralyzing grief, began weaving mandalas in the quiet of her mornings. Each thread represented a personal conflict that, once unraveled, turned pain into symbolic reconciliation.

While aging brings physical and cognitive challenges, adaptive practices can sustain this introspective encounter. Traditional methods like reflective writing can be substituted with voice recordings for those with physical limitations. Similarly, the repetition of symbolic gestures—such as lighting a candle or arranging a meditation space—acts as a bridge between the external world and the inner retreat. In Norway, elder care homes have incorporated these rituals alongside technologies like cardiac biofeedback, allowing participants to synchronize their breath and heartbeat while viewing photographs from their past—merging memory and identity in a conscious process.

Yet the greatest emotional challenge is not the absence of companionship, but the confrontation with echoes of the past: unmet aspirations, unresolved relationships, untaken paths. Jung's technique of active imagination enables symbolic dialogue with these repressed elements. One notable example involved a man in his eighties who began conversing with his younger self—a figure that repeatedly appeared in his dreams. These exchanges led him to rediscover his love of music and co-create a symphony with his grandchildren, giving new meaning to his legacy.

Creativity in the solitude of old age often emerges in unexpected ways. A study from the

MIT Media Lab showed that seniors with limited mobility developed artistic expressions using only eye movement. These "gaze choreographies," captured via eye-tracking devices, transformed emotions into visual patterns, later exhibited as testaments to resilience. This creative process evokes the archetype of the Fool or Harlequin—one who turns limitation into renewal.

Solitude doesn't mean total disconnection. On the contrary, brief, strategic interactions can enrich it. Encounters centered around essential questions—like "What beautiful thing did you discover today?"—have been shown to increase oxytocin, a hormone linked to social well-being. A program in Montreal pairing elders with young philosophers found that even 15-minute conversations generated meaningful bonds without exhausting participants' energy.

Emotional autonomy in later life doesn't imply detachment, but rather an integration of independence and connection. Neuroscience research has found simultaneous activation of brain regions linked to social pleasure and self-awareness in individuals who achieve this balance. Such capacities can be cultivated through practices like digital fasting, which promote internal observation and appreciation for the simplicity of bodily and mental processes.

Some of the most profound testimonies come from those who've turned solitude into community contribution. One 89-year-old woman, homebound, created an anonymous storytelling network—sharing mythological tales with strangers over the phone. This project not only improved her emotional well-being, but also fostered deep, momentary connections with her listeners.

The essential paradox of solitude in aging is its power to open us to the world even as we turn inward. As Jung once wrote,

"Well-inhabited silence is not emptiness, but the chamber where the soul's echo becomes a song we all share."

15. Creativity and Old Age

Creativity in old age isn't a simple revival of youthful skills—it's a cognitive transformation, where decades of lived experience are elevated into fresh, original expressions. Carl Jung observed that the collective unconscious doesn't diminish over time; rather, it deepens, becoming a vast reserve of latent symbols waiting to inspire new forms of creativity.

Neuroscience confirms this: the dorsolateral prefrontal cortex—key for divergent thinking—remains capable of forging innovative connections well into late life, provided it stays engaged in creative practice. Artists with frontotemporal dementia offer striking examples: their work often grows richer and more abstract as other cognitive functions decline, showing that creativity can thrive even at the edge of perceived loss.

Creativity in later life often feels like psychic archaeology: uncovering and recombining fragments of memory to form new, meaningful narratives. At Berlin's Gerontology Institute, older adults create sound collages mixing personal recordings with contemporary audio. This activates the left angular gyrus (linked to episodic memory) and the secondary auditory cortex, weaving non-linear stories where time spirals in rich, emotional patterns. Jung himself described a retired watchmaker who invented an "emotional chronograph"—a clock marking symbolic moments, from a postponed loss to a transformative love.

Creative blocks in old age usually stem from cultural conditioning, not a lack of imagination. Rigid definitions of "valid" art can stifle expression. To counter this, therapists use sensory "unlearning" exercises—painting blindfolded, writing with the non-dominant hand—to break patterns and explore new expressiveness. For example, "blind ceramics" workshops in Spanish care homes guide participants by touch, not sight. Brain scans show these activities strengthen connections between the caudate nucleus (pleasure) and the inferior parietal lobe (multisensory integration), fostering enjoyment in the creative process itself rather than the outcome.

In literary realms, autobiography in later life takes on an alchemical quality: more than chronicle, it becomes symbolic reinterpretation. In Toronto, a study using "quantum autofiction" invited participants to imagine alternate versions of real events—engaging the temporoparietal junction, associated with empathy and perspective-taking. This narrative method deepens self-awareness and nurtures the capacity to hold multiple realities while maintaining identity.

Art therapy has moved into transmedia territory, integrating technology and creativity. In Japan, elderly individuals with advanced Parkinson's use digital tools that translate tremors into abstract strokes. These works, displayed publicly, turn limitations into unique aesthetic statements. Brainwave analyses during these sessions reveal theta–gamma coupling—a state tied to extraordinary creative clarity—confirming that physical challenges can spark entirely new forms of artistic expression.

History offers many late-blooming creatives. Ukrainian folk artist Maria Prymachenko began painting in her fifties, weaving folklore and surrealism in bold, precursory modernist works. Physicist Freeman Dyson published influential astrobiology research in his mid-eighties—showing that conceptual creativity knows no age.

Geriatric neuroaesthetics offers further insight: when older viewers contemplate abstract art, they show increased activity in the medial orbitofrontal cortex (aesthetic appreciation) and the hippocampus (memory). Programs at MoMA encourage participants to link masterpieces with personal memories—creating personal-universal narratives.

The deeper significance of late-life creativity lies not just in the art produced, but in its power to shift cultural values. Japanese textile artist Sachiko Morimoto began weaving at 94 using seaweed fibers—challenging traditional ideas of utility and permanence. Her biodegradable textiles, designed to return to the sea, embody Jung's idea of creativity as an intentional participation in cycles of decay and renewal.

Rather than becoming introspective or sidelined, this creativity acts as a bridge between memory and prophecy. In the aging brain, creative endeavors merge the default-mode network (imagination) with executive control (discipline). This neural synergy allows elders to inhabit multiple temporalities at once—braiding past experiences into forms the future will continue to unveil.

16. The Psychic Legacy

In Jungian thought, the "psychic legacy" is a transcendent imprint that far surpasses material possessions or visible achievements. It is a lasting echo etched into the collective unconscious—an encapsulation of the individuation process, the integration of conscious and unconscious elements into the broader symbolic reservoir of humanity. Unlike tangible assets that decay, the psychic legacy resonates within archetypal structures that link generations.

Building such a legacy requires deliberate introspection and synthesis. Jung likened this to "psychic archaeology": excavating the layers of one's life to distill enduring meaning. This involves distinguishing the transient from the timeless—seeing episodic events as personal anecdotes and archetypal patterns as universal truths expressed through individual lives. By examining letters, diaries, and memories, one can trace recurring "guide-images"—symbols that shape one's narrative. Freed from personal context, these images can become metaphors shared and reinterpreted across time.

Transmitting a psychic legacy isn't limited to words. Jung highlighted the power of "liminal objects"—symbolic artifacts that bridge personal memory and collective resonance. One powerful example is a Holocaust survivor who fashioned a pendant from rusted camp wire; donated to a museum, it transformed from a private memento into a universal symbol of resilience.

When life stories become "mythobiographies", they transcend chronology to become transformative journeys. A teacher, for instance, structured his memoir around totemic animals, each representing a life stage. These symbols enriched his legacy and provided students with a metaphorical language to narrate their own struggles and aspirations.

Mentoring in later life becomes an "alchemical process" rather than mere instruction. Consider a retired physics professor who gave students river stones—each stone representing a mistake he made. At the end of the ritual, students cast them into a river—a symbolic gesture showing the value of error as a gateway to learning. This simple act conveyed a teaching philosophy that went beyond facts to embrace growth through experience.

Preparing for death can be seen as an act of "psychic sowing". Jung proposed three reflective questions:

1. "What seed have I planted that has yet to bloom?"

2. "What of my words still echoes in others?"

3. "What deed of mine will outlive my breath?"

These questions aren't for definitive answers, but to activate reflection on which facets of the self are worth sustaining. One artist, facing his final days, filled postcards with abstract lines and mailed them anonymously— each recipient interpreted them personally, extending his symbolic presence well into the future.

Historical examples show how a psychic legacy can surpass fame. Psychiatrist Takeo Doi spent his final years developing the concept of "amae"—a healthy emotional dependence—and led circles of elders sharing vulnerability stories. These oral archives now support intergenerational therapies, showing that legacy need not be grandiose; it can flourish as dialogue and human connection.

The paradox of the psychic legacy is its "anonymity": the more universal it becomes, the less dependent it is on personal recognition. Like ancient ceramics shaped by nameless potters, its enduring value lies in nurturing growth patterns beyond individual identity. Truly wise aging doesn't seek remembrance—it seeks fertility in meaning: stories, gestures, symbols that germinate unpredictably.

Rather than ending with death, this legacy is "activated in it". In Jung's final writings, he described dreams of a child molding clay figures and releasing them into the ocean—symbolizing archetypes cast into the collective psyche to be transformed by future generations. His insight:

his true inheritance lies not in books, but in others' capacity to reinvent his ideas.

A psychic legacy transcends a last will—it does not distribute possessions, but "hands down meaning-making responsibility". It transforms recipients into co-creators of a story that precedes them and survives them. The one who transmits their psychic legacy dissolves from isolated identity into an essential thread within the tapestry of human meaning—unseen, yet essential to its integrity.

17. Reconciliation with the Past

Reconciliation with the past in old age isn't simply sentimental—it's a transformative, almost alchemical process that turns painful memories into integrated wisdom. Carl Jung understood that "complexes"—emotional knots formed by experiences not fully processed—act like psychic magnets, distorting current perception by reactivating old wounds. In older age, as ego defenses weaken, these complexes re-emerge not as specters to avoid, but as bearers of overlooked truths demanding attention.

A powerful practice here is "intensified life review", which goes beyond a chronological retelling. Instead, one maps events by their emotional impact. A 78-year-old man discovered that a solo trip at age 60, once seen as insignificant, held more emotional weight for him than his divorce, previously thought to be the most defining moment. This reordering allows identity to untether from trauma and places events within a broader, more cohesive narrative.

"Forgiveness in old age" takes on new depth—not just releasing others from blame, but dismantling inner resentments that imprison the soul. Jung's "dual-mirror ritual" recommends writing a forgiveness letter to the perceived offender, then writing from their perspective, and finally burning both letters in water. One woman, using this ritual with her late alcoholic father, saw the ashes form light patterns reminiscent of childhood—reviving buried, positive memories.

Dialogue with one's past selves is also essential. The "embodied timeline" method uses objects placed on the floor to represent decades; walking through them, one re-experiences the feelings tied to each stage. A retired judge, reflecting on his young lawyer-self, felt chest tightness linked to past ethical compromises. Speaking aloud, "You don't need wins to validate your worth," he initiated internal repair that resonated beyond himself.

Dreams often become portals to unresolved past issues. Jung described a man who repeatedly dreamed of a dusty attic.

Through "active imagination", he discovered a box of broken childhood toys, symbols of a repressed creative self. Recreating them in clay healed this part of his history and restored his creative spark.

Reconciliation also means re-seeing parental figures as human beings with their own struggles—not untouchable archetypes. A "generational psychic portrait" exercise helps by exploring parents' and grandparents' emotional history. One woman, learning her mother abandoned musical aspirations under social pressure, reclaimed her mother's piano—transforming a story of loss into one of honoring dreams.

Healing rituals can also be symbolic and cathartic. A veteran, burdened by guilt for a fallen comrade, used shrapnel to create a mosaic depicting lives affected by war. Donated to a peace museum, the artwork turned his remorse into a public testament to shared human fragility.

Modern neuroscience supports these practices. fMRI studies show that "narrative reframing" of traumatic memories activates the medial prefrontal cortex and deactivates the amygdala—recontextualizing pain without erasing it. Techniques like "archetypal reframing" invite individuals to see hardships as mythic chapters. One entrepreneur who lost everything in 2008 likened his story to Odin sacrificing an eye for wisdom—finding cosmic meaning in personal loss.

This process doesn't erase past scars—it validates them as parts of the personal story. Like a bonsai tree that incorporates its wounds into its shape, the mature self learns to cherish its marks as proof of resilience. Jung reminded his patients that even the most damaged hearts still beat in harmony with the cosmos, showing that every life is a microcosm of the endless cycle of destruction and renewal.

18. Death

From a Jungian perspective, death is not an absolute limit but a horizon that lends depth and coherence to the landscape of life. Jung saw this final transition as a return to the collective unconscious—a realm where individual consciousness dissolves into the archetypes that shaped its existence. This process is not annihilation, but the transformation of psychic energy. What was once a self defined by time and space expands in death, reintegrating with the symbolic matrix of the universal.

According to Jung, the fear of death doesn't stem from the biological event itself, but from the resistance to relinquish a carefully constructed identity. To ease this anxiety, he proposed practices that connect the individual with timeless dimensions of the psyche. One such exercise is the visualization of a "psychic family tree," which helps transcend the sense of finality by imagining roots that reach into ancestral pasts and branches that extend into possible futures. This mental image of continuity beyond the individual promotes a gradual release from the fear of disappearance.

In dreams and visions, archetypes associated with death—such as the Traveler or the Threshold Guide—often emerge to assist in this passage. A man with a terminal illness described recurring dreams of a ferryman who asked him to "lighten the load." Inspired by these images, he began giving away his most meaningful possessions, each accompanied by a letter explaining its symbolic value. This act not only lightened his physical and emotional burdens, but also allowed him to transform the agony of dying into a conscious and meaningful legacy.

Emotionally preparing for death requires reshaping one's personal story into a coherent whole—a process Jung referred to as existential syntax. To support this, he recommended creating a "book of paradoxes," a journal in which one records the unresolved contradictions of life. Confronting these dualities—such as "I failed professionally but succeeded in love"—helps to understand that coherence doesn't lie in eliminating opposites but in embracing them as complementary pieces of a greater pattern.

Cultural beliefs about the afterlife, more than literal truths, hold a shared psychological value: they offer symbolic frameworks for processing transition. Jung viewed texts like the "Tibetan Book of the Dead" ("Bardo Thödol") not only as spiritual guides, but as manuals for navigating the layers of the psyche as the ego begins to dissolve. These active metaphors serve as inner maps in moments when certainty fades.

Personalized rituals can be powerful tools for confronting the nearness of death. One woman, nearing the end of her life, created a dynamic farewell altar. Each day, she placed an object representing a meaningful role—like a work medal or wedding ring—and consciously gave herself permission to let it go. This act not only facilitated gradual detachment but also transformed her final days into a celebration of releasing identity masks.

Pre-death dreams often feature symbols of deep transformation, such as chrysalises or seeds buried underground. Jung told the story of an elderly man who dreamt of climbing a mountain whose rocks became transparent when touched. The dream symbolized his fear of being seen in his barest essence, stripped of the achievements that had defined his life. By working with this image, he was able to face death with radical authenticity, shedding the weight of external expectations.

Legacy, as a form of transcendence, need not consist of great deeds; it can reside in simple, intentional acts. An octogenarian gardener cultivated a seed bank of wildflowers, labeling each packet with human virtues like "Resilience" or "Ephemeral Joy." By distributing them, his passing became a symbolic and ecological gesture: every blooming flower a living lesson in life's continuity beyond the individual.

Individuation in the face of death involves what Jung called a psychic doubling—becoming both actor and observer in life's final drama. In his own near-death experiences, Jung described perceiving himself as a character in a universal myth, where each decision and experience took on meaning within a larger cosmic pattern. This outlook doesn't erase the pain of parting, but places it within a context that transcends the personal.

To integrate the reality of death into everyday life, Jung aligned with the Stoic concept of "amor fati"—lovingly accepting one's fate—but added an essential nuance: the importance of actively dialoguing with the inevitable. One suggested practice is the "horizon dialogue." At sunset, contemplate the setting sun as a metaphor for your own life, and note in a journal which parts of the day would be worth repeating eternally. This habit does not deny death; it uses it as a reminder to live with greater intention and depth.

Death, seen as a horizon, neither closes nor confines existence—it illuminates it. It is a constant reminder that all conscious life dances between the transient and the eternal. In this balance, human beings achieve their greatest dignity—not as masters of fate, but as attentive weavers of the threads that bind each individual experience to the vast tapestry of humanity.

19. Sexuality and Intimacy in Old Age

From a Jungian perspective, sexuality in old age is not merely a fading echo of youth, but a transformed force—capable of transcending the purely genital and expressing itself as a symbolic language deeply rooted in the psyche. For Jung, libido was not just a sexual drive but a vital energy that could take many forms: creativity, spirituality, contemplation. In later life, this energy moves beyond its original expressions—focused on reproduction and physical pleasure—to nourish deeper dimensions of being. Thus, a 68-year-old man might rediscover desire, not through sexual acts, but in a fascination with painting mythological nudes, where eroticism is sublimated into a dialogue with archetypes of timeless beauty. This metamorphosis does not imply repression but a shift toward expressions that integrate memory, imagination, and transcendence.

The stereotype linking old age with asexuality oversimplifies and distorts this complexity. Societies often project onto the elderly their own fears of physical decline, confusing hormonal changes with an absence of desire. Yet research conducted in matriarchal communities—like the Mosuo in China—reveals a different reality: in these cultures, postmenopausal women serve as sexual mentors, guiding the young in the art of eroticism as a path to self-knowledge. Jung might have interpreted this phenomenon as a manifestation of the archetype of the Mature Hetaira—a figure embodying erotic wisdom independent of fertility. In contrast, many Western societies tend to suppress this potential. Hormone therapies often aim to preserve a genitalized version of youth, neglecting to facilitate new forms of intimacy that extend beyond intercourse.

In old age, intimacy is redefined as a deep connection rooted in mutual recognition of one another's shadows. Unlike youthful infatuation, which relies on idealized projections of anima and animus, relationships between older adults are forged through the sharing of psychic scars and the wounds that have shaped their lives. At the C.G. Jung Institute in Zurich, one clinical exercise invites couples to create "body collages": on paper silhouettes, they place images symbolizing emotional wounds and unfulfilled desires. By overlapping these collages, they discover patterns of complementarity—silences that resonate, fears reflected in the stories of the other. This archaeological intimacy finds, in the cracks opened by time, the raw material for a renewed eroticism. Here, touch does not seek possession but affirms shared existence: "You're still here, and so am I."

When sexuality shifts from performance to ceremony, the archetype of the Mature Lover emerges. This figure does not repeat learned scripts but improvises with the slow, conscious rhythms of the aging body. In a case shared by analyst June Singer, a 72-year-old widower began dancing the tango in front of a mirror. It was not mere entertainment: each step, each pause for breath, became a conversation with his physical limitations. The tango became a way of loving his own bodily history. Interestingly, neuroscience supports this transformation: studies show that practices like slow dancing activate brain areas associated with pleasure with an intensity comparable to that of intercourse in youth.

The physical challenges of aging—such as vaginal dryness or erectile dysfunction—are not merely obstacles, but invitations to reinvent. Jung proposed a powerful tool: symbolic amplification. One prostate cancer patient who had lost erectile function dreamed repeatedly of an underground river lit by fireflies. Upon exploring this image, he realized his sexual energy was shifting from the genital to the creative. He began sculpting erotic figures in clay, transforming suffering into a meaningful artistic experience. Far from being a dysfunction, his illness became a crucible in which pleasure took on new forms.

The integration of anima and animus at this stage enables a sexuality that is androgynous and whole. A man of 80 may find in the act of caressing his wife's face an experience as profound as intercourse in his youth. Likewise, a 78-year-old woman may discover in tantric massage a gateway to the sacred feminine—

without seeking climax. These experiences do not deny the body but expand its possibilities: the skin becomes a parchment of tactile memory, and breath a bridge to psychic connection. Sensory bioerotic workshops in Swedish senior homes stimulate often-overlooked areas like the soles of the feet or the ears, helping the elderly rediscover pleasure through simple, meaningful stimuli.

Eroticism in old age can be seen as a culmination of the individuation process Jung described—where Eros and Logos merge into an integrated expression. The journal of an octogenarian nun illustrates this integration: through poetry, she channeled her libido into mystical ecstasy. In her verses, Mary Magdalene and Christ converse as alchemical lovers, transforming desire into a language of spiritual union. For Jung, this would not be an act of sublimation but of erotic sanctification—the same impulse that once sought physical union now yearning to merge with the archetype of the Eternal Beloved.

Elderly sexuality challenges simplistic notions of activity or abstinence. Longitudinal studies show that those who maintain some form of sexual life—whether through intercourse, erotic poetry, or mindful self-exploration—experience significant neurological and psychological benefits. One participant described her orgasms as "gentle waves that reconcile body and soul," showing that pleasure in this stage is not extinguished—it is reinvented.

Each wrinkle and scar of the aging body tells the story of a desire that persists and evolves. Sexuality in old age is not a sunset, but a different kind of dawn: Eros endures, transmuted, like a fragrance that lingers in the air long after the candle has burned down.

20. The Archetypal Family in Old Age

In later life, the family becomes a symbolic space where traditional roles—once rigidly defined—adapt and transform, giving rise to deeper and more meaningful dynamics. Carl Gustav Jung observed that the collective unconscious finds fertile ground in family structures, where each member represents complementary facets of a shared psychic narrative. In this context, the elder, now free from the immediate demands of child-rearing, assumes the role of a weaver of meaning. Their mission transcends protection or provision— they are tasked with deciphering the patterns that have shaped the family's story. A striking example can be found among the Navajo elders, who perform memory ceremonies by drawing intricate genealogical trees in the sand. These not only trace biological relationships but also reveal symbolic and spiritual connections across generations. Far from being a folkloric relic, this ritual echoes Jung's view of the family as a living system of symbols in constant reinterpretation.

This shift in parental role confronts the elder with a paradox: to guide without imposing, to observe without judging. Research from the Heidelberg Institute of Gerontology suggests that octogenarian parents who master this balance show increased activity in brain regions associated with emotional regulation during interactions with adult children. This neuropsychological development reflects the ability to approach family conflicts as metaphors for deeper psychological processes. For instance, a dispute over inheritance can become an opportunity to explore core values passed down through generations. In this context, the technique of mythological reframing—used in Jungian family therapy—interprets contemporary tensions through universal myths. A conflict between siblings over caregiving duties might be viewed through the lens of Cain and Abel—not to reinforce rivalry, but to illuminate inherited patterns and open paths toward reconciliation.

Grandparents, as cultural mediators, play a vital role in bridging generations. They act as translators between seemingly disparate worlds—decoding the language of their grandchildren while passing down oral traditions that ground them in their roots. In Japan, a contemporary example reflects this reciprocity: elders teach programming to young people, while learning the art of haiku in return, creating an exchange that nourishes both intellectual and emotional growth. Studies from Kyoto University show that such interactions stimulate neurogenesis in brain regions related to memory and adaptability, benefiting both older and younger participants. The Wise Old Man archetype, far from being a passive symbol of wisdom, is reimagined here as a dynamic bridge between tradition and innovation.

Unresolved family traumas require deep, almost surgical attention in this stage of life. Jung proposed a method called "dream constellations," which involves collecting dreams from multiple family members over a period and analyzing recurring images. In one documented case, three generations dreamt repeatedly of runaway horses. Upon exploration, the symbol revealed a buried trauma of forced migration. A symbolic reenactment of the escape—where grandchildren played the roles of ancestors—transformed the trauma into a narrative of resilience. This not only reconciled the family with its past but activated neurobiological mechanisms associated with healing transgenerational stress.

Rituals in old age also take on a transformative function. Beyond conventional celebrations, families can design ceremonies where participants bring objects that symbolize inherited family roles or expectations. Through symbolic acts—such as burning, burying, or transforming the items—these objects become the centerpieces of stories about how legacies have been fulfilled, challenged, or reinterpreted. A study in "The Journal of Family Psychology" found that such rituals strengthen emotional bonds and reduce stress levels, fostering greater integration of mind and body.

When analyzing family conflicts through a symbolic lens, it's essential to identify the dominant archetypes at play. A controlling mother may embody the Hera archetype, while a rebellious son might represent Prometheus. Jungian therapy encourages imaginative dialogues between these archetypes to diffuse tension and restore balance. For instance, a symbolic conversation between a Prometheus who challenges and a Cronos who fears change may reveal shared anxieties about time, relevance, and familial identity.

The legacy elders leave their descendants goes far beyond material inheritance. Ethical codes passed down through daily experiences—like cooking with grandchildren or sharing stories of hardship—are deeply engraved into the collective memory. Studies show that this multisensory transmission, which combines words with actions and emotional context, activates brain networks related to learning and reward, helping ensure these values endure across generations.

Welcoming new members into the family, such as sons- or daughters-in-law, can be enriched through rituals that symbolize the fusion of lineages. Inspired by Samoan practices, such rituals might invite the newcomer to contribute an object representing their heritage, which is then integrated with family heirlooms in a ceremony celebrating unity in diversity. Anthropologists note that these symbolic acts foster harmony by integrating the unfamiliar without erasing family identity.

In old age, the family becomes a living organism where the individual and the collective interweave. The elder who understands this no longer tries to control the family drama, but instead focuses on facilitating the transformation of its members. Each person, by confronting their own inner challenges, contributes to the growth of the whole—shaping a system in which generations find their place and meaning within a shared narrative.

21. Spirituality and Transcendence

In the final stage of life, spirituality emerges as a language that transcends the personal to touch the universal. Carl Jung understood this awakening as a deep immersion into the symbolic layers of the psyche—a dialogue between the Self, the internal totality, and the collective unconscious, stripped of the ego's masks. At this stage, spiritual experiences are not illusions but manifestations of an inherent capacity to weave meaning into existence. Studies in neurotheology show that older adults often experience states of integration between self-reflection and spatial awareness—phenomena associated with transcendent connection and reflected in brain patterns that unify symbolic and emotional processing.

The distinction between institutional religiosity and lived spirituality takes on special relevance in old age. While the former may offer a refuge of certainties, the latter becomes a space of transformation where rituals become encounters with the sacred. Research in settings such as monasteries and elder care facilities suggests that those who engage in rituals with mindful intention experience neuroanatomical changes that reinforce the connection between body and mind. Practices like prayer, when approached as meditative acts, turn each gesture into a bridge to deep memories and meaningful emotions—elevating routine into sacred presence.

Spirituality in this stage does not imply detachment from the body, but rather its reintegration into a symbolic process. Jung recounted the case of an elderly woman whose joint pain, when approached through active imagination, transformed into inner images of luminous roots. This type of approach—mirrored in many current therapeutic practices—allows physical suffering to be reinterpreted as a narrative of transformation. Brain scans show that such interventions not only reduce pain perception but also stimulate symbolic integration processes that foster a deeper understanding of one's life.

Narrative and symbolic tools become particularly powerful in the search for meaning during old age. Methods like reverse autobiographical writing—from the present back to the past—can uncover unexpected links between life events and archetypal patterns. This process not only brings coherence to memory but also reshapes one's view of the future, now connected to the eternal. Similarly, everyday rituals performed with intention turn mundane activities into ceremonial acts, allowing the elder to experience the sacred within the ordinary flow of life.

As time horizons narrow, the need to find meaning encompassing the whole of life becomes more intense. Jung proposed essential questions for exploring this dimension: What torments and fulfillments have shaped me? What have I inherited? What will I pass on? Recent studies show that such reflection activates neural networks that integrate memory and symbolism, producing a sense of overarching coherence. The meaningful objects that emerge—a notebook, a piece of jewelry, a childhood keepsake—become tangible witnesses to the act of making sense of a life.

In old age, mysticism can take on sensory forms that defy expectation. Documented cases of synesthesia in older adults with hearing loss show that voices or chants may be experienced as colors or textures, suggesting the brain's ability to reorganize itself toward spiritual perception. Far from being anomalies, these experiences reflect a reframing of perception that enriches the individual's relationship with the transcendent.

Preparing for death can be approached as a symbolic process that connects elders with their spiritual dimension. Rituals such as the "psychic will" or exercises that structure memories and emotions into tangible objects offer frameworks for reconciling the past and embracing what lies ahead. These practices not only support acceptance of the inevitable but also foster cognitive-emotional integration, reinforcing a sense of wholeness at life's threshold.

Contemplating nature as a mirror of one's own existence becomes a powerful tool for reconciling with the cycle of life and death. Pilgrimages to decaying natural environments—such as forests in decline—invite participants to reinterpret their personal aging as part of a larger cycle. These experiences not only reduce fear of death but also generate a profound sense of belonging to a cosmic whole.

In elder communities, contemporary technologies have opened new pathways for exploring spirituality. Personalized virtual realities allow for the creation of inner temples that reflect each person's unique psychic landscape. When shared in groups, these experiences create a collective tapestry of meaning that transcends physical limitations and offers a sacred space for deep connection.

The spiritual awakening of old age does not seek final answers but opens space for fundamental questions with renewed depth. Like a mature tree that houses entire ecosystems within its bark, the elder becomes a space where multiple truths coexist and nourish one another. This transcendence is not a final goal, but an atmosphere that surrounds existence—casting light, even into the darkest corners, with the reflection of the eternal.

22. Healing the Parental Complex in Old Age

Healing parental complexes in old age can be understood as a transformative process in which deeply rooted emotional wounds become sources of self-knowledge and reconciliation. Carl Gustav Jung identified these complexes as emotional cores shaped by early relationships with the mother and father figures. Though they originate in childhood, these structures persist in the unconscious, influencing behavior and relationships well into adulthood. In later life—when external demands ease and the nearness of death prompts reflection on one's legacy—these complexes often reemerge with renewed intensity, demanding to be understood and integrated as part of the final stage of individuation. This is not merely about revisiting the past, but about confronting unconscious patterns that have long shaped dynamics of authority, care, and autonomy.

Dreams in old age often offer privileged access to these deeper layers of the psyche. It's common for elders to dream of their long-deceased parents appearing in emotionally charged scenes. One striking case involved a man who repeatedly dreamt of his mother waiting for him at a train station, beside a clock frozen at the time of his birth. Through active imagination, he began to engage in dialogue with this dream figure and discovered that the stopped clock symbolized his feeling of arrested emotional development—stemming from adult responsibilities he had taken on as a child. This therapeutic process helped him mentally reframe those inner images, transforming the sense of stagnation into a narrative of growth and reconciliation.

Recognizing and transforming the inner parental figures does not mean idealizing the past, but rather gaining a more nuanced understanding of the unconscious projections that shape emotion. Jung proposed a form of "emotional archaeology," involving the mapping of inherited emotional connections—not just as events, but as archetypal patterns. A woman who identified a legacy of emotional distance among the women in her maternal line reinterpreted this narrative by weaving a tapestry in which each thread represented both the wounds and the strengths of her foremothers. This symbolic act allowed her to reframe her family history, integrating previously unseen qualities and achieving greater emotional cohesion.

Reevaluating one's own parenting role in old age often brings a confrontation with what Jung called the "shadow of caregiving." Some discover that despite their best intentions, they unconsciously repeated family patterns they had consciously rejected. One man, who prioritized providing materially for his children—mirroring his own emotionally distant father—engaged in a healing ritual by writing confessional letters and burying them beneath a tree in his garden. Years later, as the tree bloomed, the decomposed letters had become nourishment for the roots, symbolizing the transformation of guilt into renewed connection with his descendants.

Parental complexes can also be seen as echoes of stories that extend beyond those who carry them. In a therapeutic group, several participants reenacted their ancestors' lives in short plays based on family documents. One man, while portraying his immigrant grandfather, came to understand that the man's perceived coldness concealed a deep sorrow over exile. By emotionally reinterpreting these behaviors, the participants were able to relieve generational patterns of resentment and guilt. Recent studies show that this kind of therapeutic role-play activates brain areas linked to emotional reevaluation, decreasing fear-based reactivity.

Rituals that combine emotional evocation with symbolic integration techniques have proven effective in healing deep parental wounds. One woman, burdened by the lifelong stigma of being an "unwanted child," used a technique inspired by EMDR therapy. She visualized her deceased mother knitting a shawl using colors that represented her own personal qualities. This visualization, paired with bilateral stimulation, enabled a reprocessing of the memory and the integration of a new affective circuit into her emotional system.

Integrating the positive aspects of internal parental figures requires moving beyond a focus solely on pain. Jung encouraged the use of meaningful objects as bridges for reconciling with past contradictions. A war veteran, placing his father's military medal next to watercolor paintings the man had secretly created during retirement, rediscovered a shared creative bond. This shifted his perception from resentment to gratitude. Such acts help surface overlooked facets of parental relationships, transforming pain into insight and growth.

These reconciliation processes yield not only internal healing but also tangible changes in current relationships. Studies on heart rate variability have shown that older adults who resolve inner parental conflicts experience more balanced and authentic family interactions. These shifts promote greater reciprocity and reduce patterns of control or dependency, fostering deeper, more meaningful connections between generations.

Even after the physical death of one's parents, dialogue with their archetypes continues as part of ongoing psychic work. A 90-year-old woman, by writing and recording conversations with her inner mother, was able to distance herself from a critical voice she once attributed to her parent—recognizing it instead as a projection of her own perfectionism. This practice not only provided emotional relief but also activated brain regions linked to self-regulation, as confirmed by recent neurological studies.

Healing parental complexes in old age does not mean erasing the past, but transforming it into a resource for the present. As Jung noted, this process creates space for the Wise Elder to emerge—rooted in earth enriched by the lived experiences and lessons passed down from one's progenitors.

23. Nature as a Mirror

To the aging eye, nature reveals a symbolic language in which every element becomes a reflection of the soul's inner processes. Jung observed that old age opens a perception deeply attuned to the environment, dissolving the boundary between observer and observed. This connection allows the organic rhythms of the landscape to serve as metaphors for psychic experiences. In the twilight of life—when the body demands a slower pace—details once unnoticed gain significance: moss creeping through the cracks of stone evokes persistence; the serene motion of mature sunflowers illustrates the wisdom of slowly turning toward the light.

The theory of "unus mundus" finds fertile ground in old age, particularly through synchronistic experiences involving ecological patterns. In Norway, a group of older adults documented correlations between bird migrations and pivotal life moments: cranes flying overhead during funerals, or swallows nesting during recovery from illness. These events, interpreted as messages from the collective unconscious, are supported by neuroscientific findings. Individuals who perceive such meaningful coincidences show heightened activity in the fusiform gyrus—a brain region crucial for recognizing patterns. This suggests that the aging brain becomes more finely attuned to the implicit language of nature.

From this perspective, gardening in later life transcends recreation and becomes a transformative experience. Therapeutic horticulture projects have shown that elders often cultivate plants that symbolize their life stories. One Holocaust survivor revived a grapevine he had hidden as a child, while a former ballerina designed an herb garden whose movements mirrored a waltz. These practices awaken a "vegetal memory" that links the gardener to narratives rooted in the soil. Microbiome research reveals that elders who tend these gardens develop hand bacteria similar to those found in the earth they care for, demonstrating a symbolic and physical integration between human and environment.

Dreams also serve as a channel through which nature communicates psychic truths. An analysis of hundreds of dream accounts revealed that older adults frequently dream of moving water—an image Jung interpreted as a symbol of vital flow persisting beyond physical decline. A retired fisherman described visions of fish caught in nets of ice, reflecting his resistance to the limitations of aging. Inspired by these images, he sculpted fish from wax and melted them in periodic rituals, symbolizing emotional release and reconciliation with change.

The theory of natural fractals provides a framework for understanding these connections between psyche and landscape. Repetitive patterns in snail shells or tree branches have a calming effect on older individuals, reducing oxidative stress and promoting psychic integration. In Japan, programs use visual projections of fractal structures—ranging from cellular to galactic—generating a sense of cosmic unity that enhances emotional well-being.

The perception of time also shifts for elders when contemplating slow geological changes or forest growth. A Swiss Alpine study showed that observing minute patterns of erosion in mountains increased tolerance for bodily change. This expanded temporal awareness, measured in cognitive tests, correlated with greater gray matter in the parietal lobe, an area associated with sensory integration.

Across cultures, rituals that connect with natural cycles help elders cope with physical decline. In Mapuche ceremonies, elders bury teeth alongside blue corn seeds, symbolizing the potential for bodily loss to give rise to renewal. Similar urban practices—such as creating ephemeral mandalas from fallen leaves—invite reflection on the beauty of transience while fostering acceptance of aging.

Neuroaesthetic research into aging shows that natural landscapes activate specific brain areas in elders. For instance, viewing autumn colors stimulates the medial orbitofrontal cortex—linked to existential evaluation—

suggesting that elders interpret natural cycles not just as sensory stimuli but as metaphors for life itself.

The practice of "ecological dialogue" adds a therapeutic dimension to this connection. Guided by Jungian psychologists, elders choose elements from the natural world as symbolic mirrors of their lives. One 82-year-old man recorded imaginary conversations with an ancient olive tree, projecting onto it the scars of his life. After a year, not only had his self-acceptance significantly improved, but the olive tree also showed unusually dense growth rings—an unexpected parallel in organic time.

These findings align with the theory of extended biophilia, which proposes a deep interdependence between human aging and ecosystemic rhythms. Recent studies show that elders in sustained contact with nature synchronize their internal cycles with lunar and seasonal patterns, enhancing expression of genes related to longevity. Nature acts not only as mirror, but as active agent in physical and emotional well-being.

The perception of the aging body as a microcosm of nature has inspired unique artistic projects. In Finland, life-size body molds seeded with mosses and lichens symbolize cycles of decay and regeneration. Participants reported reduced fear of death and a deeper sense of connection to the earth—effects supported by biological markers such as lowered cortisol levels.

Ultimately, nature, with its continual flow and transformation, becomes a teacher of old age. Its lesson lies in accepting change without resistance, adapting without losing identity. As Jung wrote:

"The oak does not envy the stream its movement, nor does the moss aspire to the pine's height. Each fulfills its cycle in the great dream of the earth."

24. Time and the Psyche

Old age reveals a temporal paradox that escapes the linearity of clocks. While the body yields to the inevitable advance of "chronos"—the sequential, objective measure of time—the psyche journeys through the realm of "kairos", where moments are valued for their symbolic density rather than duration. Carl Jung interpreted this transformation not as decline but as a profound reorganization. The aging brain, no longer consumed by the urgency of productivity, develops a distinct temporal sensitivity: the capacity to inhabit multiple layers of time simultaneously. Neuroimaging studies show that older adults activate distributed networks—including the hippocampus, medial prefrontal cortex, and angular gyrus—when recalling memories. These neural connections give rise to a memory that is not a static archive, but a dynamic fabric in which past and present are in constant dialogue.

One notable example is that of an octogenarian linguist who, after losing track of the current date, began recording her experiences using three tenses: nighttime dreams for the past, sensory perceptions for the present, and intuitive visions for the future. Far from being disoriented, her writing reflected a psychic integration of time as a multidimensional flow.

The theory of "ghost times" offers insight into how certain psychological periods remain alive in the psyche long after they've ended chronologically. This explains why older adults sometimes relive youthful conflicts with renewed intensity. Jung documented cases of individuals who, after retiring, experienced anxieties identical to those felt on their first day of school. These reactivations are not mere reminiscences but unresolved complexes rising to be integrated as life nears its completion. Therapeutic techniques using biographical timelines help uncover such recurring patterns. A striking case involved a 78-year-old man who discovered that his fear of flying was tied to a childhood terror of climbing trees—both linked to the archetype of the fall. By exploring these connections, he transformed his phobia into a fascination with mythic images of flight, particularly in Norse mythology.

The temporal experience of aging challenges the classic division between memory and projection. Studies by the Max Planck Institute revealed that older adults spend more time than younger people engaged in free association, weaving together memories, current perceptions, and future visions into a coherent narrative. This process is reflected in symbolic weaving traditions—such as Mapuche grandmothers intertwining yarns of different colors to represent decades of life—creating a loom where distant episodes converge into a unified design. In the brain, this integrative capacity activates the Papez circuit, responsible for emotional and temporal coherence, generating a sense of existential fulfillment that softens the fear of finitude.

Temporal rituals in old age acquire a transformative dimension. Beyond traditional birthdays, ceremonies like the "lunar rebirth" emerge, in which participants reflect on a specific year of their lives in alignment with lunar phases. One retired astronomer, for example, burned old scientific notes during full moons and planted seeds from long-lived trees such as sequoias and olive trees. This act symbolized his shift from a precise, quantitative concept of time to a cyclical, contemplative view—reconciling his analytical mind with a deeper rhythm.

Although neurogenesis slows with age, it supports Jung's view of time as a multidimensional experience. Existing neurons grow extensions that connect previously unlinked brain regions, enabling associations between distant life events. In one experiment, adults over 70 associated childhood scents with recent experiences more quickly than younger participants. This phenomenon, known as "future memory," allows elders to project upcoming scenarios based on symbolic patterns rather than rational plans. A retired general, for instance, used his antique coin collection to foresee geopolitical trends, linking each coin to recurring historical cycles.

In the dream realm, old age evokes what Jung called "dreams of eternity": experiences where time expands or contracts in extraordinary ways. A review of over a thousand geriatric dreams revealed frequent imagery of nonlinear time—such as clocks running backward or landscapes where seasons coexisted. These dreams express the unconscious's attempt to convey the relative nature of psychic time. One 90-year-old woman dreamt of swimming in a river alongside past and future versions of herself. When she painted the scene, she recognized the currents as symbolic of the many life rhythms flowing simultaneously within her.

The essential challenge of this stage is to dwell in the paradox of time: to accept the finitude of chronological time while experiencing the timelessness of the Self. Practices like "three-time meditation"—which involves consciously breathing through the past, present, and future—synchronize theta and gamma brain waves, associated with memory and heightened awareness. This state allows elders to explore their biography as a spiral, where each turn gathers and transcends the one before it.

Even cognitive decline can reveal symbolic potential. In cases of frontotemporal dementia, the loss of chronological awareness is often accompanied by heightened symbolic sensitivity. One former watchmaker, for example, who could no longer read the hour, began drawing clocks where numbers were replaced by personal symbols—a stolen kiss at 20, the birth of a grandchild at 9. This unique temporal language, far from a deficit, expressed a profound understanding of time as a collage of meaningful moments.

Old age radically transforms our relationship with time: linearity gives way to lived experience, and chronological succession becomes a depth rich with meaning. Each moment is felt as a microcosm of echoes and possibilities—a living integration of past and future within the ever-unfolding present of being.

25. The Sacred Autumn

The "sacred autumn" is a metaphor Jung used to describe old age as a season of spiritual and psychological harvest—when the fruits of a lifetime of experience and reflection reach their ripeness and prepare to nourish future generations.

This sacred autumn is not an ending, but a time when the psyche—after decades of germination, blooming, and maturation—arrives at its fullest expression. In this phase, life is contemplated as a whole, without clinging to what was lost or what will never be. Jung described this stage as the culmination of an alchemical process that defies natural laws—where what was scattered becomes a coherent whole, and absence reveals fertile spaces for new growth. Here, the linear perception of time so typical of youth dissolves into a cyclical understanding: every wrinkle on the skin traces a story; every silver hair is woven into the fabric of memory. In this transformed aging, the years do not merely pass—they are transfigured into symbols, rich with meaning.

During this cycle, archetypes that once competed for dominance within consciousness begin to reconcile. Figures such as the Wise Old Man and the Witch, the Hero and the Orphan, become integrated within a single prism, carved by the soul's tides. Thus, when someone at seventy returns to a passion abandoned in youth, it is not a repetition of the past, but the closing of a life circle—where the creative impulse of childhood enters into dialogue with the introspection of maturity. Jung intuited this phenomenon as a form of individuation, and contemporary neuroscience supports it: research shows that in the aging brain, increased connectivity between hemispheres enables emotional and cognitive synthesis. Functional MRI studies reveal that older adults resolve moral dilemmas by simultaneously activating regions linked to judgment and empathy— illustrating how wisdom arises from the balance between these faculties.

In contrast, modern society's obsession with productivity often misreads this slower integration as decline. Yet in cultures such as the Kaluli of Papua New Guinea, elders are revered as bridges between the tangible and the spiritual—tasked with transforming experience into myth, to nourish the collective unconscious. A UNESCO analysis of communities with gerontocratic structures found significantly lower depression rates among elders, highlighting that wisdom thrives in contexts where its communal roots are recognized.

The modern challenge lies in repairing the disconnection between the biological and symbolic dimensions of aging. Hyper-technological approaches tend to reduce aging to a list of deficits—bones losing density, neurons slowing down, hormones decreasing. Against this limited vision, Jungian thought offers an alchemical perspective: physical conditions can be seen as metaphors for psychic states in need of transformation. In some Swiss clinics, for instance, sculpture is used as a therapeutic tool for patients with arthritis—inviting them to model their pain in clay. Beyond physical relief, this practice creates a profound sense of meaning, activating neural networks linked to resilience and emotional adaptation.

In this framework, death is not a failure or a boundary—it is the final phase of individuation. Preparing for it does not mean resignation, but learning to let go consciously—like trees that release their leaves in autumn to preserve their essence through the winter. Rituals such as planting forests with trees that will mature long after their planters are gone reframe finitude as an act of hope and legacy. Neurological studies show that individuals who engage in such rituals experience increased brain activity in areas related to temporal integration, demonstrating how the connection between past, present, and future enriches the experience of transcendence. Death, as the final horizon, does not close or confine existence—it illuminates it. It becomes a lasting reminder that all conscious life dances between the transient and the eternal. And in that balance, the human being reaches their greatest dignity—not as master of fate, but as an attentive weaver of the threads that connect each individual experience to the vast tapestry of humanity.

Malcolm J. Austin

The End

About the Author

Malcolm J. Austin (born in 1975) is an American author and spiritual teacher known for his work on New Thought philosophy and personal development. Born and raised in Boston, Massachusetts, Austin developed a deep interest in spirituality and the potential of the human mind from a young age.

A graduate in Psychology from Harvard University, Austin began exploring various philosophical and spiritual traditions, including New Thought, positive psychology, and mindfulness practices. His quest led him to study with several contemporary spiritual teachers, ultimately synthesizing their insights with the core principles of New Thought.

Austin is a prolific writer and speaker, sharing his teachings through books, seminars, and digital platforms. His teachings emphasize the power of creative visualization, gratitude, and the transformation of limiting mental patterns as keys to achieving financial success and abundance. He is a firm believer in the mind's power to shape reality and in the existence of universal laws that govern the manifestation of our desires.

He is also known for integrating elements of modern neuroscience and quantum physics into his prosperity teachings, aiming to bridge contemporary science with the spiritual principles of New Thought. Austin maintains that many principles of success and abundance are grounded in both ancient wisdom and recent scientific discoveries.

Throughout his career, Austin has trained numerous students in his techniques of visualization and manifestation, building a global community through online programs and in-person retreats. His ideas on the connection between mind, energy, and prosperity continue to inspire a new generation of spiritual seekers and conscious entrepreneurs.

www.ingramcontent.com/pod-product-compliance
Lightning Source LLC
Chambersburg PA
CBHW061519050726
47593CB00002B/654